FEARLESS WRITING

RESEARCH PAPER
GUIDE

STEP-BY-STEP INSTRUCTION FOR MIDDLE-SCHOOL WRITING

Written by Penny Dowdy
Copyright © 2007 by Spark Publishing

Flash Kids is a trademark of SparkNotes LLC

Spark Publishing
A Division of Barnes & Noble
120 Fifth Avenue
New York, NY 10011
www.sparknotes.com

ISBN-13: 978-1-4114-9753-5
ISBN-10: 1-4114-9753-8

For more information, please visit *www.flashkidsbooks.com*
Please submit changes or report errors to *www.flashkidsbooks.com/errors*

Printed and bound in China

1 3 5 7 9 10 8 6 4 2

NOW THAT YOU'RE IN MIDDLE SCHOOL, ARE YOU WORRIED about the difficult writing projects your teachers are assigning? Does the thought of sitting down to write an essay or paper fill you with dread? Don't be fearful—BE FEARLESS! This Fearless Writing book will help guide you through the ins and outs of preparing for, writing, and revising your very own research paper. Are you excited? You should be!

Writing is different from most other school subjects. In fact, some would say that writing is MORE FUN than most anything! Unlike math or science, writing does not require you to memorize formulas or equations. There are no clear-cut right and wrong answers here. What you will find, however, is a chance to express your thoughts and opinions through writing. Believe it or not, writing can be a good time!

The more you write, the better writer you will become, so practice, practice, practice! By writing in your free time, you will become more skilled, and those school assignments won't seem so bad after all. Check out the *Fearless Writing: Research Paper Workbook* for extra practice with research paper writing. Here are some ideas to help you practice writing on your own:

Keep a journal in which you record your thoughts daily.
Write letters to friends and family members.
Write your very own autobiography—the story of your life.

You hold between your hands the key to your new life as a fearless writer. Your days of dreading those writing assignments are over.

LET'S BEGIN!

TABLE OF CONTENTS

CHAPTER 1
WHY DO WE HAVE TO WRITE RESEARCH PAPERS?

It's an autumn day, and you head to your desk in history class. Other students are coming in and seating themselves, too. The teacher enters and greets everyone from the chalkboard. It seems like a perfectly normal school day. Then your teacher says something that sends chills through your body:

"Today, we're going to talk about a research paper that you'll need to finish by the end of the grading period."

The students all groan. It seems like you're all in for a long and painful process, but it doesn't have to be that way! Writing a research paper can actually be an interesting and fulfilling experience. Sure, you have to do it for part of your grade in the class. But along the way, you'll pick up skills that will help you with other schoolwork, and even help you succeed after graduation and throughout your life. You could call it a "Write of Passage." A research paper also gives you the chance to find out more about a topic that you are interested in. You will take new facts you've uncovered and combine them with your personal insights and conclusions. Finally, you'll have a research paper that is as unique as you are!

Do you feel like the research part of the paper is some unnecessary torture made up by teachers? Well, if you think about it, research is done anytime someone asks a question and then searches for the answer. Sometimes it's as simple as finding a number in a phone directory. Many times, though, it requires a lot of searching through books, websites, libraries, and research that other people have done. Also, finding the answer might involve making connections between bits of information that other people haven't noticed. In other words, research often leads to new discoveries!

Keep in mind, too, that almost everything we rely on every day came from research. Our cars are safer to drive. Buildings are taller and stronger than they were decades ago. We know more facts about the planets and the stars. Every time you read a book or try a new recipe, you're benefiting from someone else's research. There was someone who asked, "How do I make this better?" or "What happens when I do this?" Then that person did the research to find out. Aren't you glad?

HOW TO SUCCEED

A successful research paper is well written and contains both facts from established sources and your own convincing arguments. This doesn't happen by accident. It takes hard work and good organization, among other things. Here are some important things to remember.

READ AND FOLLOW DIRECTIONS

It may sound obvious, but many students rush into a research paper before they clearly understand what their teacher wants. Does it have to be a certain number of pages or words? What is the deadline? Can information from the Internet be used? Is there a list of topics from which you have to choose?

If the teacher's instructions are not clear, ask for specific information before you get started! Also, go ahead and ask other questions that the teacher may not have addressed. For example, if you are told that the research paper has to be 10 pages, does that mean single-spaced or double-spaced? Typed or handwritten? Is it okay to write 20 pages instead? Clearing up these details now will save you headaches later!

MAKE A PLAN

Have you heard the saying, "He who fails to plan, plans to fail"? It's good advice for any project, but especially a research paper. There's so much information to look for and so many decisions to make about what to keep and what to ignore. Of course, there's also only a certain amount of time to pull it all together. Later chapters in this book will cover in detail how to find information, how to organize it, and many other topics—but it all starts with a plan, even if it winds around like a garden path or you hit a dead end or two along the way.

Your plan will help you answer some crucial questions: Is the topic I chose interesting to me? Is the topic too broad or too narrow? Are there resources available to find the information I need? Your plan might also include specific goals. For example, you might set a deadline that by the third week you'll have finished most of your research. These are just a few examples of things you might include in your plan. You'll find help in later chapters to figure out how to make a plan of your own.

DON'T PROCRASTINATE

You can probably think of many reasons not to get started on your research paper. Some of these reasons might be genuine, and some might be silly, but all of these reasons—or excuses—have the same effect: They waste time that you could be using to get the paper done!

It's understandable, though, and you're not alone. Even experienced researchers can feel a bit overwhelmed by the task. The first key to research paper success is just to get started.

CHAPTER 2

WHAT'S THE BIG IDEA?

Okay, you might be feeling a bit overwhelmed, but you just need to know what your first step will be, and here it is: The best place to start your paper is choosing your topic.

First of all, what is a topic? A *topic* is the main idea—or the main subject—of the paper. Everything in the paper is there to support the topic, or "Big Idea." For example, if you were writing about Will Rogers, your topic might be about his acting career. You could write about how his career began, the films and plays he was in, and the roles he performed. Later in this chapter, you'll learn how to focus your topic to make it more interesting to your reader (and easier to write the paper). An effective paper starts with a well-defined topic. It holds the reader's attention—whether that reader is a classmate, your teacher, or anyone else.

The first and most important rule of picking a topic is to pick one that interests you. Interesting topics are simply easier to research and write about. You might even want to choose a topic that you've written about before, maybe from a different angle or in greater depth. On the other hand, you might want to choose a topic that you're not too familiar with but are interested in learning more about. Just choose one that can hold your enthusiasm for the time you'll need to write the paper.

You won't always have a choice of the topic that you'll be writing about. Your teacher may already have a list of topics or ideas for you, or perhaps you have to stick to the subject of your class. If that's the case, talk to your teacher about the things that interest you, and together you can define your topic.

One warning: When you start working on your paper, you might find that your research takes you in a different direction than you intended. You could start looking at your original topic in a different way, and that's okay. If this happens, you can just adjust your topic to fit your research.

Okay, time to choose! Let's look at the many different ways you can come up with a topic that's interesting to you and your teacher.

BRAINSTORMING YOUR IDEAS

Have you ever noticed that sometimes you come up with your best ideas when you're not focusing so hard on them? The first method for finding a topic does a similar thing, as it allows you to let loose ALL of your ideas about a topic to see what gems turn up. *Brainstorming* is a method of writing down rough thoughts, ideas, and questions about the topic or subject you already have in mind. You give yourself a certain amount of time (such as 10 minutes), and write down anything you can think of during that period. The ideas could be single words, phrases, or sentences. Don't worry about misspellings or other errors. And don't worry if your ideas look messy or unorganized or just plain out there. After you finish brainstorming, you'll look more closely at what you wrote.

Remember the Will Rogers idea? Here's an example of how brainstorming could help someone zero in on a topic about his life and career. You would start with a blank sheet of paper, and write ideas and questions that come to you as you think of them.

He was a writer	He was a celebrity	From Oklahoma?	Alive during the World Wars
He was funny	Was he in the movies? On stage? A politician?	Oklahoma City airport is named for him. Was he a pilot?	Was he a soldier? If he was a pilot, did he fly in a war?
Did he write for newspapers or magazines, or did he write books?		Oklahoma makes me think of cowboys and Indians. Was he either a cowboy or a Native American?	

From this sheet, you now have many questions about Will Rogers that can be answered with a little research. You also have some idea about the different things he did in his life. Digging deeper into a few of these points may lead you to your research topic.

FREEWRITING

Freewriting is a lot like brainstorming, except your ideas are written down as a paragraph instead of as a list. When you freewrite, you also set aside a short amount of time, but you write about a broad topic as if you are writing an essay. However, your freewriting exercise won't really look like an organized essay. The important thing is to continue writing for the whole time you've set aside. Don't stop for spelling errors. Don't try to find the perfect words. Don't even worry if your ideas make sense. If you're stuck at any time, just write "I'm stuck. Can't think of anything" and continue. At the end of your five or ten minutes, read what you've written. Cross out everything that doesn't seem important. Then focus on the remaining ideas. Even after crossing out the unimportant stuff, you should have a few ideas you can build on. Here's an example of a freewriting exercise:

Amateur Baseball

I live in a small town, so we don't have a major league baseball team, or a minor league team. But we do have a lot of amateur baseball teams. These teams are organized and have their own league. It's fun to watch them play every Friday and Saturday night. My dad plays on one of the teams. He practices twice a week right after work. Each team gets sponsored by a local business, like a bank or a grocery store so they can buy uniforms and bats and gloves. I wonder if anyone has written about these teams. Local newspaper? I can't think of anything to write. Right now, I play in a youth league. When I'm old enough, I might join one of these teams. There are probably amateur teams in other towns. I wonder if my dad's team has played them? I wonder if our mayor can get a minor league team to move to our town?

WELL, WHAT DO YOU KNOW? CREATING AN AUTHORITY LIST

You've probably heard the advice, "Just write what you know." While every good writer uses careful research, good grammar, and an eye for detail, he or she usually starts with some understanding of the topic. Think about it: Ernest Hemingway could write the classic war novel *A Farewell to Arms* because he experienced war firsthand. Stephen Hawking can interest us in physics and astronomy because he has devoted his career to studying those subjects.

Not that you necessarily need to be an expert to write about a topic, but it may be a worthwhile exercise to use your own life experience or interests to discover a topic you can explore. To do this, you create an *authority list* of subjects you are interested in, such as hobbies, sports, or history topics. Then, you can make this list more specific by figuring out how much you know and care about these topics.

Your authority list can be a table with rows and columns. Each row can start with a broad topic, and then each column to the right can list more detailed information about the subject. Using this method, you can narrow down a broad topic into a more focused one. Remember that an authority list should include topics that you already know something about. You shouldn't have to do any research to make one! It can get as detailed as you wish. After completing it, you may find a topic you want to explore further. Here's an example of how an authority list might look:

Baseball	Great pitchers	Nolan Ryan's no-hitters
		Greg Maddux
	Great hitters	Willie Mays vs. Babe Ruth—who's the best?
		Hitters from 50 years ago vs. hitters from today
American Civil War	Difference between armies, navies	Which army had better generals?
		Iron and wooden ships during the Civil War
	Differences between economies	Southern slavery and farming
		Northern industry
Hurricanes	Parts of hurricane	Eye wall—what happens inside
		Spiral rain bands—severe weather
	Tracking hurricanes	Different radar and satellite images
		Reporting information to public

CLUSTERING

Clustering is a way of working out and displaying your ideas in the form of a map, with ideas connecting to similar ideas. This method can be good for people who prefer reading maps instead of written directions. While brainstorming and authority lists are linear, clustering allows your ideas to spread over a page in different directions. You might expect the opposite result, but clustering can help you examine how your ideas might relate to one another and figure out how much you have to say about a topic. And since you might be re-drawing and re-arranging ideas, it's wise to use a pencil. Here's an example of clustering, using the topic of robotics:

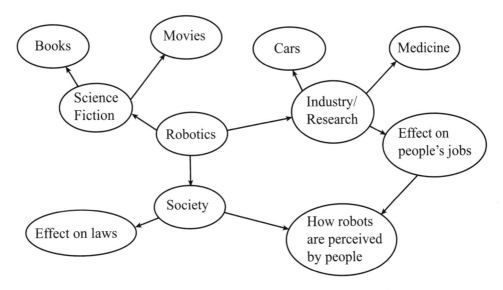

THE LIBRARY AND THE INTERNET

If you're still stuck for a topic to research, there are two places you can visit for vast amounts of inspiration and information: your local library and the Internet. In fact, many libraries also offer free Internet access. At the library, you should seek out the reference librarian. This person is an expert in finding information of all kinds, especially in a special type of resource called *reference books*. These include dictionaries, encyclopedias, guides, and dozens of other specialized books.

Reference books are very helpful because they can include information from hundreds of sources for a specific topic. For example, if you want to write about the American Civil War, you can use the *Encyclopedia of the American Civil War*. What's more, at the back of these types of books, you can find a list of all the resources the editor and writers used. This can lead to more books for your research! If you use reference books, however, make sure you check out the most recent edition available. Chapter 4 will go into more detail about these valuable materials.

Another excellent source of topic ideas is *periodicals*. This is a big category of publications that are printed on a regular basis. For example, you probably know that magazines are published weekly or monthly. Journals are usually published monthly or quarterly (four times a year). You should be able to find a magazine or journal dedicated to any topic you can think of—automobiles, skateboarding, tae kwon do, carpentry, you name it! Your library should have many old issues of these periodicals. Magazines and journals are also a good way to catch up on the latest news and developments in a specific field of interest.

The Internet also has a huge amount of information. You have to be careful, though, with the information you find there. Can it be trusted? Is it accurate? Chapters 4 and 5 go into more detail about how to closely examine and use Internet sites.

TIPS ON SUCCESSFUL RESEARCHING

No matter where you search for ideas or topics, here are some general tips to keep in mind:

- As you read books, journals, and Internet sites, take note of unique words or phrases that are used in that area of study. Almost all topics of research—such as medicine, sports, or history—have their own terms and phrases. These unique words will be the *keywords* you can use to search for more information in other books and sites.

- Write down the author, title, and publication information for every book you read, even if you're just browsing. Also make a note of the book's *call number*. That's the unique Dewey decimal number somewhere on the cover of the book, often the spine. Taking these notes will save you a lot of time if you need this information again. For websites, make a note of the URL address. This can be found in the address bar at the top of the browser.

- Remember that every book that you read, and even some websites, will have a bibliography listing all of the resources it used. These are great lists to find other sources for your research.

THE "JUST RIGHT" TOPIC

If you used one or more of the methods from earlier in this chapter, you should have a good topic in mind. However, the topic might be too broad. To make it appropriate for a research paper, you have to use this topic to ask a question or explore an issue. In a way, this is a lot like a hypothesis in scientific research. You make a statement or ask a question about your topic, and then try to answer it. This statement or question should be one sentence that describes the main idea of your paper. For example, consider this topic: *blue jays.* That's a pretty broad topic, so you have to narrow it down to something more specific: *migration of the blue jay during winter.*

That helps to narrow the topic. However, for a research paper, you need to make a statement or ask a question about it. This twist will be the basis of your research. Some possible questions could be:

Has global warming affected the winter migration of blue jays?

How are blue jay migrations tracked by scientists?

Do blue jay migrations change every year? If they do, why and how?

TOO BROAD OR TOO NARROW?

When the topic you've chosen is too broad, you may feel like you've bitten off more than you can chew, so to speak. You look on the Internet or in the library for information about your topic, and you find many books or websites about it. In this case, too much information is a bad thing! When this happens, you might spend too much time going through all this information and not enough time writing your paper. On the other hand, you may have a different problem: too many ideas about how to research your topic. In this case, the paper won't be focused on any one idea, and it may be difficult for someone to read and understand. Either way, the quality of the research paper will suffer.

Here are some informal tests you can use to determine if the topic you've chosen is too broad. First, search your library's card catalog for your topic. If you find hundreds of books on this topic, it's probably too broad. In the same way, check out the magazines and journals your library carries. You may find dozens of articles and stories that have already been written about your topic. Of course, these books and magazines might have some helpful information to include in your research paper, but you will still need to narrow your topic before deciding which material to read. The same test can be applied using any Internet search engine. If you get thousands of "hits" from a search of your topic, most likely there's too much information out there.

Naturally, a narrow topic has the opposite problem of a broad topic. With a narrow one, you can't find enough information to guide your research. The same methods mentioned above can be used to determine if your topic is too narrow. In general, if you can only find one or two books in your library that mention your topic, then it's probably too narrow. In the same way, an Internet search may only turn up a dozen or so hits.

Here's another test that might help: Count the number of words in your topic statement or question. If your topic can be stated in only five to seven words, it might be too broad. On the other hand, if it takes you more than a dozen words to describe the topic, it might be too narrow. For example, here's a topic that may be too broad: *What is the life cycle of a butterfly?* Whereas, this topic might be too narrow: *How is the life cycle of the monarch butterfly affected by mild winter temperatures?*

Since these are unofficial tests, they may not work for every single topic statement or question, but in most cases, they'll help you figure out if you need to steer it in the right direction.

REFINING THE TOPIC SO IT IS "JUST RIGHT"

So how do you shape a topic idea into one that is not too broad or too narrow? There are a number of ways to do this, but basically you need to develop your topic idea further.

QUESTIONING

In the first part of this chapter, you decided on the topic for your research paper—the Big Idea, remember? This may have been a few words or a sentence describing what interested you. To make it a topic worth researching, you need to ask yourself some questions about it. These questions will help you develop a statement to direct your research. This statement is also called a *thesis*.

Think of yourself as an investigative reporter! When writing a news story, a reporter asks the same kinds of questions to get the necessary information. All of these questions start with *Who? What? Where? When?* or *Why?* For example, if a reporter is at the scene of a car accident, he or she might ask:

Who saw the accident happen?

What did the police say at the scene?

Where was the passenger taken?

When will we know if the driver is okay?

Check out how these questions can help define your topic statement, or thesis: Say you enjoy fishing and swimming in a nearby lake, so your chosen research topic is the effect of pollution on the lake. You can use the reporter's toolbox of questions to approach that topic, but you can take it one step further: Ask questions with specific "functions." Look at the types and examples below. Some of these questions may sound similar, but they are actually different ways of looking at the topic and can lead to different answers.

DEFINING QUESTIONS (HELPFUL FOR A TOPIC THAT IS TOO BROAD):

What causes lake pollution? Local businesses? Visiting tourists? People who live nearby?

Why is lake pollution an important issue?

How can the pollution issue be described or explained?

COMPARISON QUESTIONS (HELPFUL FOR A TOPIC THAT IS TOO NARROW):

How is the lake's pollution similar to or different from a nearby lake?

How has another community handled a pollution problem?

RELATIONSHIP QUESTIONS:

What is the cause of the lake's pollution? Chemicals? Organic material? Junk that people have thrown away?

What are the future consequences of the lake pollution?

Who suffers from the effects of lake pollution?

OBSERVER OR "FIRST-HAND" QUESTIONS:

What do local residents think of the pollution?

What has the local government done about the pollution?

TOPIC CROSS

Believe it or not, you can actually "visualize" the main ideas of your topic, using a *topic cross*. In this method, you arrange words and phrases around your topic in such a way that your true area of interest stands out from the rest. Let's look at an example of this, once again using the lake pollution topic.

The first step is a little more brainstorming. Spend a few minutes listing words and phrases that come to mind when you think about your topic. You may come up with phrases such as these:

Health of fish and plants	Health of people using lake
Effect on tourism	Are local businesses affected?
Where pollution comes from	Local government reaction
What do residents think?	Is pollution a common problem in the area?
Can the pollution be cleaned up?	Do other communities have this problem?

From your brainstormed list, decide which words and phrases are most interesting. Then write them down as a column in the middle of a sheet of paper. This is the vertical part of the topic cross. Write the general ideas toward the top of the column, and the more detailed or specific ideas toward the bottom. Leave space between each item.

What do residents think?

Local government reaction

Health of fish and plants

Health of people using lake

Where pollution comes from

Effect on tourism

Can the pollution be cleaned up?

Are local businesses affected?

Is pollution a common problem in the area?

Do other communities have this problem?

Look at the list to determine what looks interesting. Which topics in this list will be too broad or too narrow? Choose one area of interest, then write words and phrases that relate to that item so that they form the horizontal axis of the topic cross. In this case, let's say the idea "Health of fish and plants" looks interesting, so this is the idea we will focus on.

What do residents think?

Local government reaction

Tests on water   Check with local wildlife experts.   Talk to people who fish in this lake.

Old photos of lake?   Health of fish and plants   Do animals get food from lake?

Inventory of plants and fish?   Newspaper stories about fishing tournaments?

Health of people using lake

Where pollution comes from

Effect on tourism to the area.

Can the pollution be cleaned up?

Are local businesses affected?

Is pollution a common problem in the area?

Do other communities have this problem?

After using the methods of Questioning and Topic Cross, you may decide that any of these would be a good research topic:

The effects of lake pollution on fish and plant species

How a local community is solving its lake pollution problem

Long-term effects that lake pollution has on local tourism

Look for a common thread or idea that runs through your best ideas. Describe them clearly (remember—not too broad and not too narrow), and you have a topic statement to work from. After you are satisfied with your research topic, there's one last step: Get your teacher's approval. This may not be required for the assignment, but it's still a good idea. Your teacher can let you know whether your idea is "just right" or still needs work.

CHAPTER 3
SO MANY PURPOSES, SO MANY PAPERS

In this chapter, you'll think about the question *Why?* Why is the sky blue? Why do cats always land on their feet? Why do socks disappear in the dryer? We won't actually be worrying about those larger questions, but you will learn how to answer this question: *Why am I writing this research paper?* In other words, you will find your "purpose." The *purpose* of writing is the reason you are writing—whether to inform, explain, or persuade—and that knowledge will help you decide what type of paper you need to write.

WHY AM I WRITING?

You will not always get to choose the purpose of your research paper. Oftentimes your teacher will tell you your purpose. For example, if your assignment is something like "Compare and contrast two American presidents," then you know that you will be explaining, and you should follow the guidelines for writing a compare-and-contrast research paper.

However, if your assignment is something vague like, "Write a research report about a branch of science," you have decisions to make. Not only do you need to choose the topic but also the purpose of the paper. If you don't decide on a purpose, your paper will easily lose focus. For example, you may start out informing the reader about the U.S. space program, but then get off course and start trying to persuade the reader that more funding should be given to space exploration. Changing gears like this will most certainly bring your grade down!

After you are sure of your purpose, be sure you also know whether your teacher has assigned the *type* of paper or whether it is up to you to decide. And, once you do decide, make sure the paper stays that type and keeps its purpose from beginning to end.

THE PERSON WRITING

When you write research papers, don't use first- or second-person pronouns. You will sound more like an expert when you avoid words like I, we, and you.

For example, look at the following sentence:

> *I'll tell you about Mark Twain's life.*

Now compare it with this sentence:

> *Biographers have written much about Mark Twain's life.*

YOUR PURPOSE: DESCRIPTION

As you can probably imagine, descriptive research papers will contain lots of factual information. It's okay to spice up your paper with adjectives and adverbs, too—just be sure that the words you use are based in fact. For example, this is a good example of a descriptive sentence: "The hills of Costa Rica are covered with lush, green plants."

This sentence, on the other hand, is not a good example of a descriptive sentence: "The green hills of Costa Rica are the most beautiful in the world."

Can you see how these sentences differ? The first sentence includes descriptive writing that is not opinionated at all. But the second sentence sounds like it's conveying the emotions and opinions of the author. Your description should give a very clear explanation or description without providing your specific views on the subject.

Remember that you are explaining, too. You may include definitions, illustrations, photos, and statistics. Of course, also give plenty of examples. However, don't just list them—the person reading your paper could simply read your sources and get the same information! A good descriptive paper brings together information that isn't found in one place, or it makes connections that the reader wouldn't make on his or her own.

PLANNING YOUR DESCRIPTIVE PAPER

You can use the clustering tool from the last chapter to plan your descriptive paper. First write your topic in the center of a page. Place supporting information in circles that branch out from the topic. Details and examples can branch out even further.

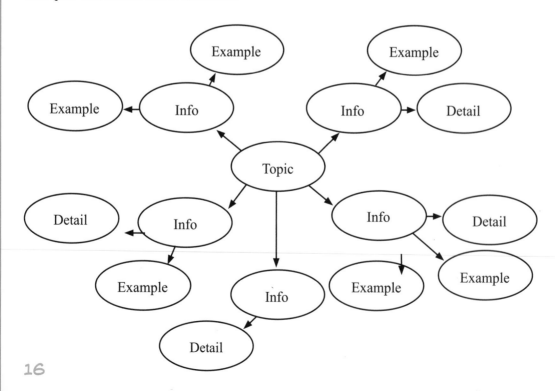

Concept maps are not specific enough for writing the actual paper, but they do give enough detail for you to know if you have enough information from which to write. You can spot ideas that need to be developed further or in more detail.

Let's go back to our friend Will Rogers. Here is the information you may already know about him, in concept map form:

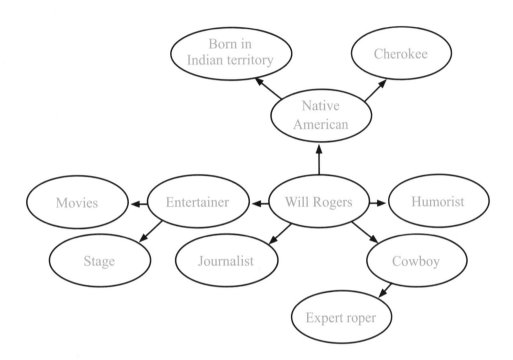

From the map, you can see that you need to find out more about Rogers's career as a humorist and a journalist, as those circles don't have any details or examples.

Another way to plan a descriptive paper is to use a flow chart. Flow charts are helpful for planning a paper that should be presented in time order, as these charts show the order of events. A biography is a great example of a paper that should be written sequentially, since it makes more sense to read about a person's life in time order. Papers on history topics may also be written this way, especially if you are looking at how the subject changes over time.

Here is what a blank flow chart would look like:

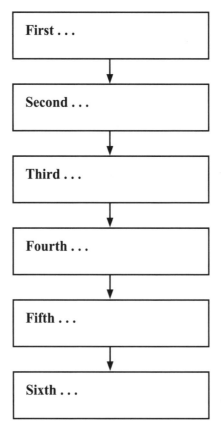

What specific topic you've encountered recently could be put into a flow chart? That's right—the life of Will Rogers! This is how it would look:

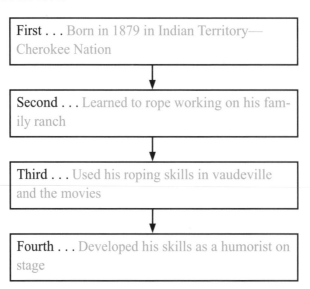

When you write a descriptive paper that uses sequence to organize the writing, remember to use *transition words* to lead the reader from one idea or step to the next.

YOUR PURPOSE: PERSUASION

A persuasive paper uses facts and statistics to convince the reader of an opinion or to take some sort of action. It is not objective, like a descriptive paper. In a persuasive paper, the writer definitely takes a side. However, the topic is presented in a way that is not emotional.

When you choose a persuasive topic, make sure there is some disagreement behind it. Think of it like this: A paper arguing the need for playground equipment in parks isn't much of a paper if everyone agrees that the park needs playground equipment. Who would read it if there was no controversy? Choose a topic that has at least two clear, opposing sides.

CAUTIONS ABOUT PERSUASIVE TECHNIQUES

There are many ways that writers try to convince readers of their side of an issue. If you were writing a commercial, you could use any one of them. For a research paper, however, there are some persuasive techniques you need to avoid.

BANDWAGON

The bandwagon technique tells people to think a certain way because "everyone else does." This technique is not based in fact, but uses a fancy form of peer pressure to sway someone's opinion.

EMOTIONAL APPEAL

This technique plays on people's emotions, often their fears. "Imagine losing everything you have because a prisoner was released from prison early . . ." Again, there is no fact behind the statement. This is not appropriate in research papers.

TESTIMONIALS

Only use sources that are experts on your chosen topic. Who really cares if a famous baseball player prefers driving an electric car? What matters is what the experts on energy savings are doing.

BROAD TERMS

Watch out for using words like *all, every, none,* or *never.* These words are very extreme and are usually exaggerations. Again, stick to facts and let them sway the reader.

NEGATIVITY

Don't use a lot of words that are clearly negative when discussing the other side of the argument. If you want to say something is wrong, be prepared to support your argument with facts. Just painting the other side with negative words is not an effective argument.

PLANNING YOUR PERSUASIVE PAPER

Since most persuasive papers consider two sides of an issue, a table like this would help you organize arguments for (*pro*) and against (*con*) the side you take:

For (Pro)	Against (Con)

You see that this kind of table doesn't give room for a lot of detail—it just gives you a way to plan your argument. Be sure that you have plenty of information on the side that you plan on taking, but also include the most likely arguments for the other side. You should be prepared to explain why those arguments are not as strong as yours.

Here is an example of what your table might look like if you were writing a persuasive paper about requiring uniforms in schools:

For (Pro)	Against (Con)
No peer pressure over what brands people wear	Buying all-new school clothes can be expensive
Easy to decide what to wear every day	Kids are not able to express themselves through their clothing
No worry about hand-me-down school clothes going out of style	
Gang colors can be eliminated in clothing	

Once you have all of your pros and cons, you can use a second organizer to arrange the information for your actual paper:

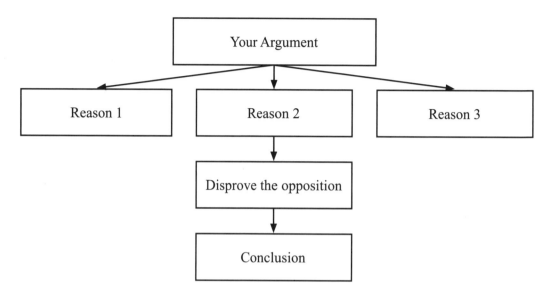

Here is how the persuasive paper about school uniforms could be organized:

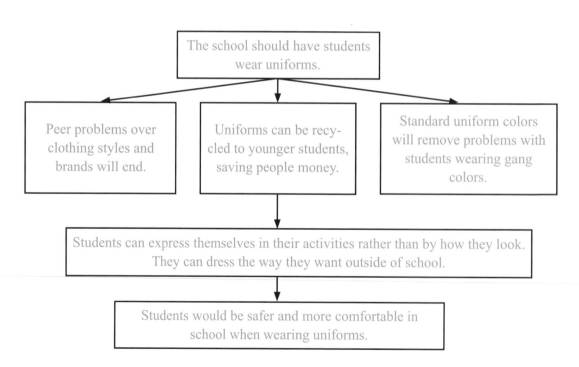

In your written paper, try to use transition words that will let the reader know when you are giving more reasons for your argument. These transitions can also prepare the reader to see why other arguments will not fly.

PERSUASION TRANSITION WORDS AND PHRASES

Here are some transition words and phrases that will help you as you write a persuasive paper:

additionally	*further, furthermore*	*the reason for . . . is*
as well	*granted that*	*therefore*
besides	*in addition*	*this is supported by*
consequently	*in fact*	*to emphasize*
despite (the fact that . . .)	*moreover*	*while it may seem that . . .*
equally important	*the evidence for . . . is*	

YOUR PURPOSE: SHOWING CAUSE AND EFFECT

A cause-and-effect paper tells about something that happens (the *cause*) and what happens as a result (the *effect*). Cause-and-effect papers are excellent for science and social studies topics. Just make sure that the link between the cause and effect is clear. Don't try to force a relationship if there isn't one!

PLANNING YOUR CAUSE-AND-EFFECT PAPER

It is rare that there is one single cause for one single effect. Instead, there are usually many causes for one effect, one cause with many effects, or even many causes with multiple effects. So the organizer you use for these papers needs to be flexible enough to hold one or many causes and one or many effects. How about a fishtail graph?

In a *fishtail graph,* the "head" is a single cause or single effect. Then the "tail" will hold the many causes or many effects, and details about each. Keep the cause or causes on the left side of the page and the effect or effects on the right side.

For example, here is a blank fishtail graph for a topic containing four causes and one effect:

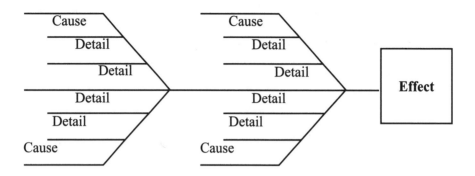

Here is the same fishtail graph filled in, for a paper on how schools have improved test scores:

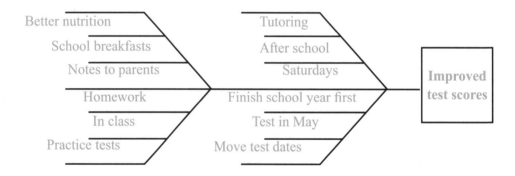

Here is a fishtail graph describing the need for students to learn Latin. Notice that the cause is singular and the effects are multiple, so the graph faces the opposite direction.

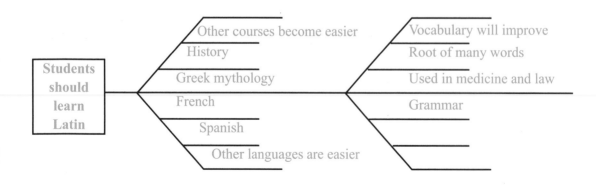

Since causes happen before effects, many papers of this type are written in sequential order. So look back on page 23 for transitional words to help your paper move from section to section. In addition, you can use some transitions specifically for cause-and-effect papers.

CAUSE-AND-EFFECT TRANSITION WORDS

Use these transition words to help you when writing a cause-and-effect paper:

as a result	*due to*	*therefore*
because	*if . . . then*	*thus*
consequently	*leads to*	*since*

YOUR PURPOSE: SHOWING PROBLEM AND SOLUTION

A problem-and-solution paper is exactly what you would expect it to be. It explains a problem and then offers a solution. It may also discuss other solutions that could have been possibilities but that had been rejected as not being good choices. Oftentimes scientific research papers are problem-and-solution papers, as well as those tackling social issues. For example, you could write a paper about the problem of vehicles speeding through neighborhoods with lots of homes and children, then present the solution that speed bumps will make traffic safer.

Much like when writing a persuasive paper, you have to be sure that your reader will agree that there really is a problem. In other words, you create a feeling of "need" so that the reader will want to read about your solution. You also have to prepare for objections to the solution—address them, and then show why they can be rejected.

PLANNING YOUR PROBLEM-AND-SOLUTION PAPER

If your chosen problem has only one good solution, then you can plan your paper using an organizer like the one on the top of the next page.

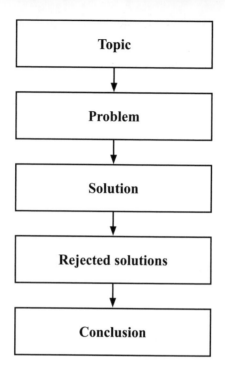

So if you were indeed writing that paper about speeding through neighborhoods, your chart would look something like this:

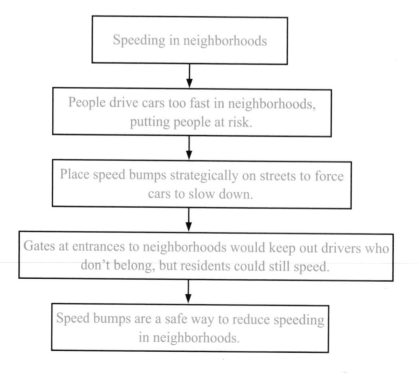

However, you could have more than one solution that you recommend. In that case, use an organizer like this:

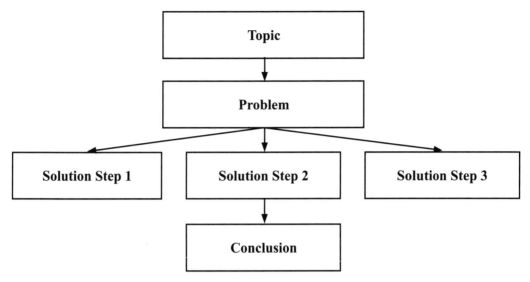

You could also add the rejected solutions before the conclusion, if you'd like. So if your paper about speeding problems had a multistep solution, your organizer might look something like this:

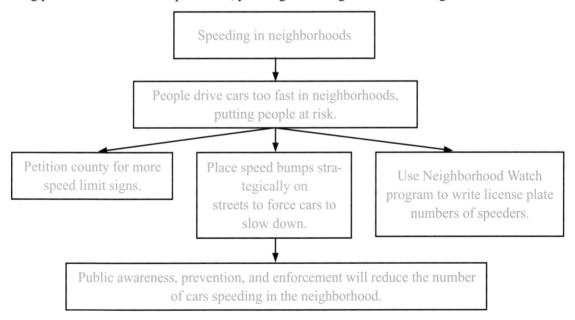

What's left? Oh, yes, the research: finding facts, experts, and statistics that really describe the problem and support your solution. As you can see, multistep solutions give you more to research. On the plus side, though, they give you plenty to write about!

Since problem-and-solution papers are similar to persuasive papers, look to the list of persuasive transition words. You will also find that some problem-and-solution papers use cause-and-effect ideas, so feel free to use transitions described in that section as well. In addition (see? a transition!), there are a few transitions perfect for problem-and-solution papers.

PROBLEM-AND-SOLUTION TRANSITION PHRASES

These phrases will help you transition from one sentence or idea to another when writing problem-and-solution papers.

One way of solving . . .

One solution would be . . .

The first solution to consider . . .

This is a problem because . . .

This problem leads to . . .

YOUR PURPOSE: COMPARE AND CONTRAST

If you don't already have a few of these under your belt, be prepared to write papers that compare and contrast two things. To "compare and contrast" is simply to identify what are the same and different about two things. You can compare books, writers, minerals, politicians, laws, and more. In some instances, your teacher will assign the two subjects for the paper. If you are able to choose the two subjects yourself, choose them *for a reason*. This means you should choose two subjects that, when compared, make surprising connections or show the reader something new.

PLANNING YOUR COMPARE-AND-CONTRAST PAPER

One of the best ways to get your ideas organized is to make a *Venn diagram*. In this diagram, you write things that are common between the two subjects in the area where the two circles overlap. The details that are different about the subjects are written in the sections of the circles that do not overlap.

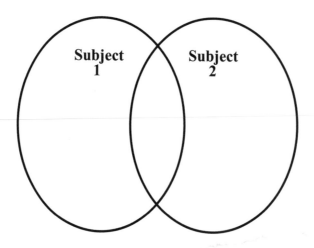

For example, if you were writing a paper comparing two alternatives to gasoline usage, your diagram might look like this:

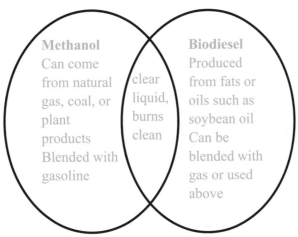

Methanol
Can come from natural gas, coal, or plant products
Blended with gasoline

clear liquid, burns clean

Biodiesel
Produced from fats or oils such as soybean oil
Can be blended with gas or used above

Another option is to organize the information in a table.

	Subject 1	Subject 2
Point A		
Point B		
Point C		

So the same alternative fuel information could be organized like this:

	Methanol	Biodiesel
Quality	Clear liquid, burns clean	Clear liquid, burns clean
Source	Natural gas, coal, plant products	Fats and oils such as soybean oil
Preparation	Blended with gasoline	Can be used alone or blended with gasoline

Then, once you start writing, you have a number of ways to present the information. You can introduce one aspect, such as the sources of these chemicals, and then tell how each subject relates to that aspect. Next, change to another aspect, and again tell how each subject relates to it.

You can write about every aspect of the first subject, and then switch to everything about the second subject.

You could organize the information by first presenting all the similarities and then the differences between the two subjects.

There is no best choice. Just decide which way will make your paper read best.

There are a lot of transitions that are especially useful in compare-and-contrast papers.

COMPARE-AND-CONTRAST TRANSITION WORDS AND PHRASES

Use these transition words and phrases when writing a compare-and-contrast paper to keep your writing flowing smoothly.

also	however	on the contrary
although	in contrast	on the other hand
both	in the same manner	similarly
but	likewise	unlike
conversely	nevertheless	while
even though		

CHAPTER 4
GO TO THE SOURCE

Okay, now you have ideas for your topic and you can see how your report can change based on your purpose for writing it. In this chapter, you'll learn how to find the information you'll need for the next step in your plan: the research. Where is this information, anyway? It could be in books, magazines, television programs, the Internet, and many other places you might not expect. All the places where you may get information for your paper are called *sources*.

Before you learn more about each type of source, here's a question worth pondering: How does information get created and end up in these sources in the first place? Let's say you're a fan of a (fictional) professional skateboarder named Tyler Austin. You just finished watching Austin win the world championship of skateboarding. It was fun to watch, but you want to know more about him and the competition. Where can you find this information? Well, it depends on how much detail you're looking for, and how quickly you want to know it.

First, we get a lot of our daily news from professional reporters, and information about a skateboarding competition would be no different. This event would probably attract reporters from television networks, newspapers, websites, and radio. These sources would provide immediate information about the event, printing or broadcasting details on the very day the event took place. You could find major details about the event and perhaps a short interview with Austin and the event organizers.

Over the next few days, you would probably find more details of the event in your local newspaper. You might also find a follow-up story on television, radio, or the Internet, including a longer interview with Austin. These stories may also include an analysis of the competition, a comparison of this year's event to previous ones, and predictions about future competitions.

In about a week or two, the story would be published by weekly magazines that cover skateboarding and other sports. They might include photographs of the event and in-depth information about the sport. These magazines may also include related stories, such as a visit to Tyler Austin's hometown or an interview with his family and friends. A magazine that is dedicated to the sport of skateboarding might devote its entire issue to covering the event. In that case, you might find an enormous amount of information not available anywhere else.

After a few months, information about the event will start appearing in books, encyclopedias, journals, and other sources that only publish once or twice a year. In these, the depth of the information might vary. For example, while an encyclopedia might include statistics, charts, a summary of the sport, and a table showing past winners, a book might include an in-depth discussion of skateboarding and more personal details about Tyler Austin. A book may also include the personal opinions and perspective of the writer, which might help you to see the sport in a different way. These books and encyclopedias would probably also include details that were already reported in newspapers and magazines, so a great deal of information about the competition can now be found in one place.

Now that you have an idea of how information makes its way into different sources, let's take a closer look at those sources and when each is most helpful. Most of them can be found in one of two places: your local library or the Internet. But there are always more sources to be uncovered!

NAVIGATING THE LIBRARY

Today's public libraries have an enormous range of sources you can use for researching. Although books make up the majority of these sources, the library also includes magazines, newspapers, films, and much more. Also, most libraries now have Internet access available to you!

When you're trying to find resources in a library, there's an easy way to do it: Just look up the appropriate call number in the card catalog. How does the library assign this number? It's based on the Dewey decimal system, a way to classify books by grouping them into 10 categories. It was invented by American librarian Melvil Dewey in the nineteenth century. The system is based on 10 classes of subjects (000–999), which are then divided into subjects that are more specific.

The call number is made up of two parts: the Dewey decimal classification and the Cutter number. One of the best uses of this system is to find books that have a similar subject. For example, if you were looking for a specific book on Native American art, most of the books on this subject would be found next to each other in the library stacks.

DEWEY DECIMAL CLASSIFICATION

The Dewey system has ten main classes, each with its own number:

000 Generalities

100 Philosophy and Psychology

200 Religion

300 Social Science

400 Language

500 Natural Science and Mathematics

600 Technology (Applied Sciences)

700 The Arts

800 Literature and Rhetoric

900 Geography and History

Each of these classes is further divided into divisions, which are further divided, as well. Each division becomes more specific. In other words, the Dewey system goes from the general to the specific. The complete Dewey tables are too long to list here, but here is a sample of part of the 700 Arts section:

700	The Arts
701	Philosophy and Theory
702	Miscellany
703	Dictionaries and Encyclopedias
704	Special Topics
705	Serial Publications
706	Organizations and Management
707	Education, Research, Related Topics
708	Galleries, Museums, Private Collections
709	Historical, Areas, Persons Treatment
710	Civic and Landscape Art

Using the Dewey tables, you can quickly find the stacks where books of a certain topic are located. For example, dictionaries and encyclopedias of art can be found together in section 703.

CUTTER NUMBERS

The Cutter number is usually the first letter of the author's last name and then a few numbers. These numbers come from a table that helps to keep the names alphabetical. What happens if there are several works by the same author? In these cases, a *work mark* is used to distinguish the author's works. The work mark is a lower-case letter that is usually the first letter of the book's title.

PREFIXES

Sometimes a call number has a prefix to indicate a special location where the book can be found. Prefixes are not part of the Dewey system and can be different at every library. However, they can help you quickly find a book that is stored in a special collection or other area. For example, many libraries use the prefix *R* or *Ref* to indicate that a book is in the Reference section.

REFERENCE BOOKS

Reference books include encyclopedias, dictionaries, almanacs, and many other specialty books. These books are usually published once a year, or every other year. Because of this, they may not have the most current information for some subjects. They are written and edited by people who are experts in a particular field of knowledge. For example, an encyclopedia covering astronomy would have articles written by astronomers, physicists, and reporters who cover developments in the space sciences.

Since most reference books cover broad topics, they usually provide only a general overview of their subject. However, some reference books may be published in several volumes that provide a lot of detail. A reference book is a good place to look for general information, as well as statistics, charts, maps, and other "visual" information. They also will have extensive bibliographies, listing all their source books and articles. This is a great place to look for more research sources.

One more tip: Most reference books cannot be checked out of a library. Check with the reference librarian to see if there are any exceptions to this policy.

GENERAL ENCYCLOPEDIAS

Since they cover so many different subjects, general encyclopedias usually have some information on every topic. They're good sources to look at first, since they summarize the main topic and recommend sources that are more detailed.

For example, a person researching tornadoes could look in *The Encyclopedia of Atmospheric Conditions*. A student looking for information on the history of pi (π) could look in *The Math Encyclopedia*.

SPECIALIZED DICTIONARIES

You know where to find definitions of common words you read and speak every day. What about words that are only used in a technical field or profession? There are hundreds of specialized dictionaries available, devoted to specific subjects and fields of study. Definitions in these dictionaries are usually more detailed than those found in a general dictionary. For example, writers needing explanations of musical terms can look in a dictionary of music.

ALMANACS AND HANDBOOKS

Almanacs are filled with charts, tables, maps, statistics, and lists, and are published once a year covering the events occurring that year. Some almanacs cover specific subjects, like the economy, while others may cover hundreds of subjects. For example, if you're wondering what team won the World Series in 1975, you'll probably find an almanac with the answer.

Handbooks are very similar to almanacs. They also provide facts in the forms of charts, tables, and statistics. They are updated more frequently, sometimes several times per year. If you receive monthly scouting reports for your fantasy basketball league, that's a type of handbook. Other types of handbooks—a scout's handbook, for instance—may be updated less frequently.

BIOGRAPHICAL REFERENCE BOOKS

Biographical reference books contain short entries for thousands of historical figures. These books may be helpful if you want to know about only the major events or achievements in a person's life. These books usually cover a specific profession or field of study, such as politics or archaeology. Others may cover a period in history, such as World War II. Many of these books can be found under the title, "Who's Who in . . ."

ATLASES

An atlas is a collection of maps or drawings that illustrate a specific subject. The most common atlases show maps of the world. Atlases are also used to illustrate subjects as diverse as battlefields, weather patterns, and other planets.

NONFICTION BOOKS

Nonfiction books are any books that contain only factual information, or tell a story that is true. They are usually written by researchers, reporters, or others who have an extensive understanding of a subject. Their length can be anywhere from 100 pages to more than 1,000.

This is a broad category, of course, and would probably describe thousands of books. You will probably get most of your research information from this type of book. Why? Because a nonfiction book probably contains much more information about your subject than any other source. In addition, it includes detailed analysis. Some nonfiction books are written by several authors, so you could also get different perspectives of your topic. Every nonfiction book includes a bibliography, so it is an excellent way to find other sources.

PERIODICALS

Periodicals are published on a regular basis, often dozens or hundreds of times per year. The most common types of periodicals you will use are journals, magazines, and newspapers. If you are researching a topic in a field that is rapidly changing, such as computers or medicine, then you may be relying on periodicals for your information. These types of publications will contain the most up-to-date information about your topic. At the same time, the information might be outdated very quickly. So if you use periodicals in your research, be sure to find the most recent issues.

JOURNALS

Journals publish current research and news in a specific field. For example, you can find journals on such diverse subjects as paleontology and cancer research. New issues are usually published once per month or three to four times per year. Journal articles are written by experts or students in the field. However, before an article can be published, it must be submitted for "peer review." Peer review is a process in which other experts make sure that the arguments and facts in the article are accurate. On account of the intensive peer review process, journals are an excellent source for accurate, up-to-date information. Journal articles also contain footnotes and bibliographies, so you easily see where the author got his or her information.

There are journals in many different areas, from preschool education to electrical engineering. A research librarian can help you find journals related to your research topic.

MAGAZINES

You are probably already familiar with many popular magazines, and you may even subscribe to some of them. Thousands of magazines are currently in publication, most of them published weekly or monthly, covering nearly every topic under the sun. There are magazines dedicated to politics, celebrities, sports, and woodworking—literally thousands of different subjects. Your local library probably won't have recent issues of all of these magazines, but they'll probably have many of the most popular. The reference librarian may be able to help you find issues they don't have.

Much like journals, magazines report on recent events and developments, but they are usually intended for a general audience. The language of the articles will not have the jargon or technical terms usually found in journals. In addition, magazine articles don't have a peer review. However, they are reviewed by editors to make sure they are accurate and clear. You can use magazines to get a summary of recent news, as well as opinions, photographs, and other general information.

NEWSPAPERS

You are probably more familiar with newspapers than with any other periodical. Newspapers are published daily, and they are an excellent source of immediate news coverage, as well as opinions, photographs, and other timely information. Just like other periodicals, the information in newspapers gets outdated very quickly. However, they cover local events and news better than any other printed source. Your local library subscribes to newspapers from around the world. So if you want to read local coverage of an event in London last week, you can probably find it! Many newspapers also keep archives of past editions on the Internet, so you may be able to access the articles without even taking a trip to the library.

FILMS AND VIDEOS

Some of your sources may be part of a film or video. Many libraries have audio-visual departments where you can access these sources. Also, many film and sound recordings are available on the Internet. Excellent examples are the American Memory Collection on the Library of Congress website (http://memory.loc.gov), and Facets Multi-Media (http://www.facets.org). These organizations give people access to thousands of films and videos, including movies, documentaries, collections, and more.

THE INTERNET

Even though your library may have thousands of books, journals, and magazines, one of the most easily accessible resources at your disposal is the Internet. The Internet can be an amazing source of information, but you have to be careful using the information you find. Think of it as the electronic version of the Wild West! No one person or organization controls the Internet, so anyone can create a website. In fact, thousands of new websites are created every day! While this has helped the fast growth of the Internet, it is therefore somewhat difficult to be sure that the information you find is accurate. This section will show you how to use the Internet to find reliable sources. We'll also look at some special websites to aid your research.

SEARCH ENGINES

As the amount of information on the Internet has increased, programs called *search engines* have been created to help you find what you're looking for. You may have heard of the most popular ones, such as Google, AltaVista, and AlltheWeb. There are also many other search engines, each with its own special way of searching. One search engine won't find everything. You may have to use several different engines to get the information you need.

Search engines use programs called *web crawlers* that automatically collect information from millions of web pages every day. This information is stored in a database. When you use a search engine, you are actually searching a database on that search engine's computers. It then gives you a list of results, or "hits," that match your search.

A search engine gives you results based on the keywords you enter, but it doesn't know what those words mean. For example, if you search using the keyword *bow*, you could get results about the bow of a ship, a bow used for wrapping a present, pages about bow and arrows, and greeting someone by bowing. You would need to add more keywords to your search to get more precise results. If you don't find what you're looking for in the first 25–30 search hits, then you may need to add more words to your search.

The search engines mentioned on page 36 are good for broad Internet searches. But you have to use them one at a time. What if you could combine the searching power of many of them in one place? This is exactly what a *metasearch engine* does. This type of search engine doesn't use its own database. Instead, it sends your search to a handful of general search engines and then combines their results into one results page. Some popular metasearch engines are Dogpile, MetaCrawler, and ProFusion.

Many search engines include advanced options you can use to improve your search results. For example, you can search only specific websites, like those ending with *.gov*. You can also search only for photos, instead of text. The features between search engines are very different. However, one powerful feature you can use with any search engine is called *Boolean commands*. You type these commands between your words to create a specific search. Here's a partial list of Boolean symbols you can use:

Command	Meaning
+	Search must include this word
−	Search must exclude this word
" "	Search must use this exact phrase
OR	Search can include either word

Here are some examples of how to use these commands. Let's say that you are searching for information on dolphins. This table shows how Boolean commands can define your search results. You can combine commands in a number of ways to get exactly the search results you want.

Search	Meaning
Dolphins + Atlantic	Search for web pages about dolphins in the Atlantic Ocean
Dolphins + Atlantic –bottlenose –spotted	Search for web pages about dolphins in the Atlantic Ocean, but do NOT include pages about bottlenose or spotted dolphins
"dolphin habitat"	Search for web pages containing the exact phrase "dolphin habitat"
Dolphin + Atlantic bottlenose OR white	Search for web pages about dolphins in the Atlantic Ocean that also include either the word bottlenose or white

RECOGNIZING RELIABLE ONLINE SOURCES

So you've found dozens, or even hundreds, of websites that may have useful information for your research report. How can you tell which sites are accurate and reliable? There are a number of questions you can ask yourself as you examine each website. Remember, the answers to these questions don't guarantee that the information is reliable, but they will help you weed out suspicious sites. If you still have doubts, ask your teacher's opinion.

Who wrote the webpage, and what is his or her background? Look for the author's name, a copyright credit (©), or a link to an organization. Also look for information about where the author works (university, company, government agency). A reliable author should include this information.

Is there contact information? Look for an e-mail address, mailing address, or phone number of the website's author. This will probably be the contact information of the organization where he or she works. A reliable author working with an established group should be willing to include this information.

What kind of organization is behind this website? Look at the three-letter ending of the website's domain. Does it end in *.com, .edu,* or *.org*? The *.edu* domain is only used by colleges and universities. The *.org* domain is used only by nonprofit organizations. These websites will probably have reliable information. The *.com* domain, on the other hand, can be used by anyone. You'll have to look at other aspects of a *.com* site to determine if it's reliable.

Why did the author create this web page? The purpose for the web page could be several things: advertising, news, opinion, humor, research, or for other reasons. You might need to look at several pages of the website to find out the purpose.

Is the information on the web page up-to-date? Look for a date at the bottom of the web page, or on the home page of the site. This might help, but you may also need to compare this information with another source, such as another website or a book, to see whether or not the information is current.

Is the information objective? This might be difficult to determine. Look at some of the facts that are given and compare them to other sources. Is there something missing or out of place? Check to see if the author mentions where he obtained his facts. Is the website showing a balanced view of the subject, or is it one-sided? Is advertising on the website separated from other information?

COLLEGE WEBSITES

The websites of universities and colleges are good places to find reliable information. Many of them publish the results of their research. You can find the names of professors and graduate students who might be willing to be interviewed for your research report. They might also help you get hard-to-find books and other source material.

Most universities specialize in specific fields of research, and their websites have excellent information about that subject. For example, the University of Virginia has an extensive amount of information about Thomas Jefferson. The University of California, Los Angeles, specializes in medical research. The Massachusetts Institute of Technology conducts research on robotics and artificial intelligence.

ONLINE ENCYCLOPEDIAS

Until the Internet came along, encyclopedias were only available as hardbound books. Some of them had dozens of volumes. Many of these encyclopedias are now available online. Some of them allow you to conduct basic searches of their database for free, but more detailed searches usually require a fee or a subscription. The information they provide should be reliable. However, you should still apply the same questions we used to examine other websites—you want to make sure the information is accurate and up-to-date. To find these sites, just use the keywords "online encyclopedia" in any search engine.

MUSEUM WEBSITES

Many museums also have websites that show part of their collections and exhibits online. Museums usually specialize in a specific field of interest, such as science, art, medicine, and other areas. They also have curators who keep up on the latest developments and issues in that field. They could be an excellent resource to further your research.

INTERVIEWING EXPERTS

Sometimes you won't find the information you need for your report in books, magazines, or on websites. There may be a local expert who knows all about the topic you're researching and can help you with your project. To get this information, you need to interview your expert. This section tells you how to arrange and carry on a successful interview.

First, contact the expert and arrange the interview about a week in advance. (Remember, a reliable website's author will provide contact information to get in touch.) You will probably meet at the expert's office or home. A telephone interview is also possible, if this is more convenient for both of you. Thirty minutes should be plenty of time to set aside for your interview.

Use a tape recorder, but be sure your expert knows that you will be taping the interview. Remember, recording a telephone call without permission may be illegal.

If possible, submit your questions to the expert in advance, perhaps in an e-mail. The expert will be able to prepare ahead of time, and may be able to get books, papers, and other resources that can help in the interview.

Prepare a list of questions, but be flexible. Write your questions in order, but leave space on your pages so that you can write down responses. Note cards are best to use for these questions. Don't be afraid to ask a question that was not written down. Try to prepare "open" questions. These are questions that can't be answered with just a simple "yes" or "no." They allow the expert to give more elaborate answers and more information. For example, instead of asking, "Were you a good student?" you could ask, "How would you describe your years of schooling?"

You might want to practice recording before the interview, to make sure your equipment is working. You should also plan to take notes of the interview. You'll be happy to have the notes in the event that your recording does not work, for some reason.

Confirm your appointment by calling the expert about a day ahead of time. Be prompt and well dressed. When you meet, introduce yourself and let the expert know a little about yourself and the report you're researching. Don't forget to let the expert know that you appreciate the time he or she is taking to meet with you.

During the interview, give the expert time to think after you ask a question. Remember, moments of silence are okay! If your subject seems to be having trouble, ask easier questions. At the end of the interview, make sure to ask, "Is there anything I didn't cover?" Also ask, "Where would you recommend I go to get more information?" The answers to these questions may lead you to valuable sources for even more information.

At the end of the interview, give the expert your name and phone number, and thank her for her time. Shake hands and let your expert know you would be grateful to hear from her if she has any more information to add.

Don't forget to write a thank-you note and mail it within 24 hours of the interview. It's better not to send an impersonal e-mail—the time it takes to send a handwritten note will show your appreciation.

CHAPTER 5
SIT DOWN AND READ!

Finding materials to use for your research paper is only the beginning of actually doing the research. You should now be ready to spend a considerable amount of time reading. That's the research part of a research paper, after all!

Your first reading task is to find out if the material you found has information you can use. This can be done with a quick read-through of the materials. Then you will read more thoroughly the materials that you decide are helpful to find the detailed information and quotes that you will use to write your paper. As you read both quickly and thoroughly, you will be taking some sort of notes to use when you sit down to write.

READING TO REFINE

Don't be surprised if your topic changes slightly as you start reading. When you get more information, you may find that your initial research question is a bit off-track. This is very common, so don't worry if it happens.

For example, your initial topic may have led you to find out why the Russians were able to beat the United States into space. Instead, you may find more information on why the Russians weren't able to get to the Moon after they sent Yury Gagarin into orbit before the United States. It's a slight difference, but it changes your focus significantly.

If this happens to you, just check with your teacher to be sure that the change is approved.

SKIM, SCAN, AND READ

The first time you read the material, you should simply skim it. All you are trying to do is get the main idea of the material, and find out if there are facts, figures, or illustrations that closely relate to your research topic. So how do you skim? Follow these few basic steps:

- If there is a table of contents, read it. Go to the chapters or sections that relate to your topic.
- Look over the chapter or section, reading all headings and subheadings.
- Read the opening paragraph.
- Read the first sentence of each paragraph.
- Look at all figures, charts, graphs, images, or maps. Read the accompanying captions.
- Read the conclusion or last paragraph of the material.

If you find that the information in the material is not what you need or what you expected, then stop skimming. Put the material aside and move on. However, don't stop at the table of contents. Sometimes writers use catchy titles to make the writing interesting, but this can be misleading to the reader if that's all you read. So skim the main reading selection, then if the information is still not related to your research topic, move on.

What's the difference between skimming and scanning? Skimming and scanning are easily confused. Skimming comes first, and is simply used to tell if the reading is important or useful. Scanning is used for finding specific information. Skimming got you to the page or chapter that has good information. Scanning is reading to find the details of that information.

Scanning is still not the same as reading to understand. Like skimming, you can do it quickly. You should scan the material that you decide might be useful from the earlier skimming. This time, though, you are looking for key words and ideas that you may want to use in your paper. Scanning saves you time, since you eliminate reading all of a selection where paragraphs may be all you need. When you find these pieces of useful information, mark the page to read thoroughly later.

So you have skimmed and scanned. Now take some time to carefully read the information that you marked as useful. Make sure you understand what the author is saying. Think about what the author says and how it fits in to your research topic. You may find you need to read a few paragraphs earlier or later than you thought to get a clearer picture of the information. It's better to do this than misunderstand the writer's ideas or words.

GETTING YOUR ACT TOGETHER

It is critical that you keep track of the information you find in your research. It all needs to be well organized so that you can find what you need later when you begin to write. If you take time and do this well, you will have an easier time writing and documenting your paper. If you take this step lightly, you will have a much more difficult time later on. Let's look at why you need to get organized at this point.

- You need to be able to find important information when you start writing.

- You need to be able to write direct quotations exactly as they appear in the text.

- You have to be able to name your experts and the sources of information when you use them.

- You might need to go back and review information you found for more details.

- You must document your research sources when you write footnotes, endnotes, and the bibliography.

PHOTOCOPIES

Probably the easiest way to record the information you have found is to make photocopies. You can copy the pages from a book or magazine, and this is especially helpful with materials that you can't take with you—like encyclopedias, journals, and other materials that libraries don't allow you to check out. Make sure you also copy the title page and the information about when, where, and by what company the material was published. If the pages you copy don't have page numbers, mark that information somewhere on the copy so you can find the information again later if you have questions.

There are a few drawbacks to photocopies. First, they usually cost money. If you have a lot of pages to copy, or many books to copy from, the price can rise quickly. Second, photocopies are big. You will have full-page size papers to manage. They are easily bent and torn, and laying them all out to plan your paper can get messy. Third, you may need more than one piece of information from a single page. You may need a system that is more flexible, where each piece of information you use is kept separate.

NOTE CARDS

Note cards are a terrific way to document and keep track of the information you find in your research. You can use whatever size is available and large enough to work with. You can even use self-stick notes in different colors as note cards. Just make sure they are large enough so that you only write on one side of the card. This makes all of your information visible at one time.

NOTE CARDS MEANS TAKING NOTES

When you take notes on note cards, you *don't* want to write down paragraph after paragraph from your source. You should write only the information that answers your research question or provides details you can use. To take notes, either:

- summarize—write a shorter version of the author's words and ideas, or

- paraphrase—write an idea in your own words, or

- quote—write the author's words exactly as they were written, and in quotations to show that the words are someone else's.

SOURCE CARDS

So let's say you are writing a research paper on the life of Charles M. Schulz, the creator of the comic strip *Peanuts*. Once you have selected your sources, you can create a note card for each source.

A source card might look like this:

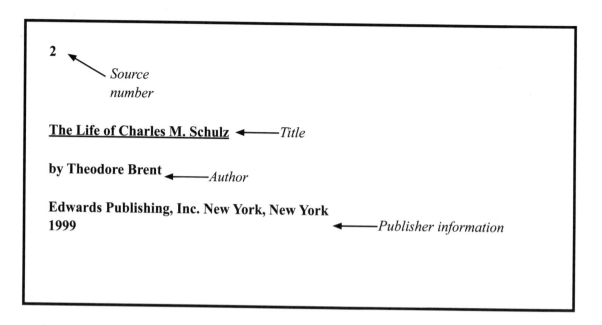

The *source number* is the number that you assign to each book, magazine, website, or resource material. You assign each different source a number so you can use the numbers on the note cards for the ideas you will use.

The *title* is the title of the book or article. You may find websites, for example, that don't have an actual title. In this case, just leave that out.

The *author* is the writer (or writers) of the book or article. Again, you may find websites, for example, that don't have an actual author listed. In this case, just leave that out.

The *publisher information* is the company that published the book or article, the location of the publisher, and the year the material was published. This is usually found in the front few pages of the book. Magazines also have publisher information within the first few pages. For websites, look for copyright information for the date of the page. Do *not* provide the name of the web developer, or the company that designed the web page. You should list the website, and if there is one, the name of the company, college, or organization that posts the information.

Here are a few more examples of source cards:

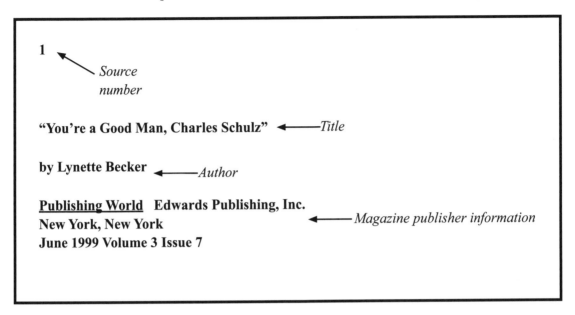

The source card above is for a magazine. Note that you need the name of the article *and* the name of the magazine. Most magazines also have a volume and issue number (often on the cover). Since magazines are published frequently, give the date shown on the cover. A source card for a journal or newspaper would look very similar to the source card for a magazine.

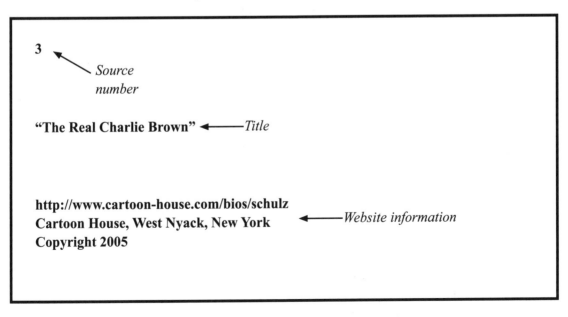

The source card on page 45 is for a website. If you can't find the information about the company, school, or organization on the page you use as a source, then go to the home page of the website (in this case, http://www.cartoon-house.com). If you can't find the information there, look for a "Contact Us" or "About Us" page. If you hunt around and can't find more information about the source, then you might reconsider using the information you found. Notice on this card, there is no author listed. If you can't find the name of the author, it's left off the card.

CREATING NOTE CARDS

Now, if you find some information that you want to use in a book about cartoonists, you can create a note card like this:

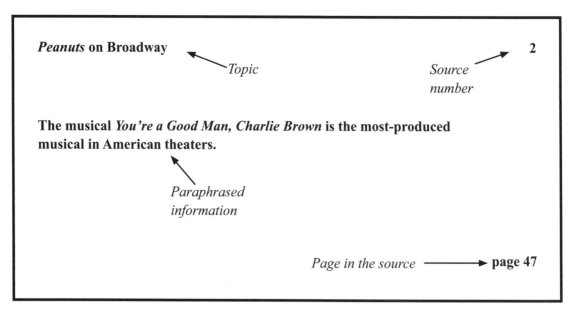

The *topic* tells the kind of information found in the source. You will decide on the name of the topic, and most of the time it is simply the main idea. After you find the information in the source, figure out with what topic it belongs. For example, if you are writing about Charles M. Schulz, you may have cards with topics such as:

- *Peanuts* on Broadway
- Schulz's life after fame
- The start of *Peanuts*
- Schulz's childhood
- *Peanuts'* popularity
- *Peanuts* on TV

The *source* is the name of the book, magazine, website, etc., in which you found the information. On our card, the source is a number. You can write the title on each card, or list your sources on separate cards like we did earlier. Number your sources on the cards, and then use the numbers on the note cards to show what information comes from which source.

Next on the card is the information that you found. In this case, the information is paraphrased, or summarized. Summarizing on the note card itself helps you ensure you don't plagiarize, or steal, the author's actual words.

It is critical that you remember to write down the page numbers on your note cards. You will need them to document footnotes and endnotes. It is also a lifesaver when you have to go back to the source to find additional information.

Here is another way you might record a note card:

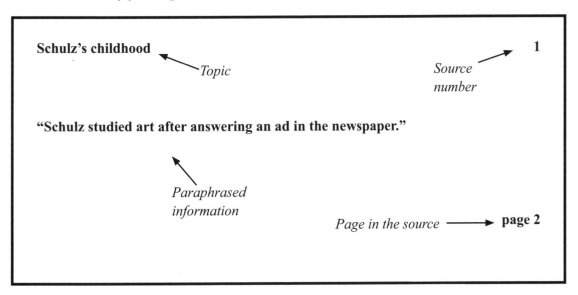

For the card above, the information was taken word for word from the source. When you do this, put quotation marks around the words.

Before you decide the card is complete, go back and reread it. Since this research is the foundation of your paper, it is important to get the information correct. Check the numbers, facts, data, and other information to be sure it is all accurate. Make sure your notes are detailed enough to make sense to you later. Don't be so brief that your notes are not meaningful when the time comes to write.

Finally, organize the cards by putting similar information together. Group the cards by the topic you wrote in the top left corner of the cards. You can color-code each topic to make finding information more visual, or bundle each topic together. Either way, when it comes time to start writing, the information for each part of the paper is together and easy to find.

ARE YOU REALLY DONE RESEARCHING?

Grouping the note cards by topic is helpful in another important way. You can see if you have enough information for each topic in your research report. If you have only one or two cards for an important point you plan on making, you know that you need to spend a little more time researching that area. If you don't have any information for an important topic in your paper, then get back to the library!

NOTE-TAKING USING A COMPUTER

So much research is done on the computer that it makes sense to take notes on the computer, too. You can do this with a word processing program, such as Microsoft Word. For example, you could make a table like this:

Source Number	Topic	Information	Page Number

Then you can keep a list of sources, just as you would with note cards. Otherwise, the way you take notes is the same.

Using the Internet in conjunction with a word processing program makes it very easy to copy and paste information directly from a website into your paper. But instructors are savvy enough to know what information is plagiarized. Most schools have policies against plagiarism that include mandatory failing grades—in some schools, you could even be expelled. Instead of caving to temptation, accept the challenge of learning something new and be proud of the accomplishment of completing the assignment the right way.

EVALUATING SOURCES

Before you scramble to write up a note card for information that you find, take time to make sure that the source is worth using. The only way your paper will carry any authority is if your sources are dependable.

ACCURACY

The first way to evaluate a source is to determine if it is accurate. In other words, does the information seem correct? If the information in one source contradicts another, then you have an accuracy problem. You also have an accuracy problem if the author of the source can't or doesn't tell where his or her information came from. There should be some sort of evidence for an author's claims, just like you will provide in your paper. Credible authors tell names of the experts they interviewed during their research. The authors will also include endnotes, footnotes, and a bibliography to back up their information. Without this information, you can't be sure that the source is usable.

If you answer *yes* to any of the following questions, your information may have a problem with accuracy:

- Does the author leave out names of sources of information?
- Does the source lack a bibliography?
- Does the author leave out footnotes and endnotes?

EXPERT OPINIONS

In some cases, the author may express an opinion on the given topic. In these instances, you need to consider the author. Is he or she an expert? An expert will have credentials, or information showing that he or she has experience in the area.

For example, if you are writing a paper about changes in automobiles over the last three decades, you could look to an expert on automobiles. Your uncle who likes cars and tinkers with them in his spare time is not an expert. An engineer who has designed cars for a major carmaker and is a columnist for a large car magazine is an expert.

If you answer *yes* to any of the following questions, your information may have a problem with the "expert" opinion:

- Does the author lack appropriate credentials?

- Is biographical information on the author hard to find?

BIAS

Information you use in your research should be objective. The author should not have an unfair interest in the information he or she writes about. The information should be fair, not biased.

For example, an article published by the oil and gas industry on the need to drill for oil in national parks is considered biased. You couldn't trust the source because it stands to gain by getting people to believe its side of the issue.

If you answer *yes* to any of the following questions, your information may have a problem with bias:

- Does the author give only one side of an argument?
- Do you notice any bias?
- Is the tone of the writing one-sided?
- Does the author stand to gain anything from the information presented?

VARIETY

It is also important to get information from many different sources. If you use information from only one author for your entire paper, your teacher will look at your research as incomplete.

You also need to make sure that your research covers all aspects of your paper. If your topic is comparing and contrasting yoga and tai chi, you can't have 10 books on yoga and only one website about tai chi. There needs to be a balance in the information you find.

If you answer *yes* to any of the following questions, your information may have a problem with variety:

- Are most of your sources by one author or source?
- Do you have many more sources for one part of your paper than another?

CURRENCY

When we talk about currency in terms of research, we're not talking about money! When you do your research, you may also need to look at how recent the information is. In some cases, the age of the information is not critical. For example, if you are writing a paper discussing the life of George Washington, it is reasonable to assume that the information published 20 years ago is still current. There may well be more current sources, but Washington's life would not have changed in the last 20 years.

However, if you are writing a paper about the role of computers in education, then current information is a must. Computer technology changes every year, so a study about the impact of computers in the classroom done in 1978 is too old to be useful.

If you answer *yes* to any of the following questions, your information may have a problem with currency:

- Does the information about your topic sound out-of-date?
- Has your topic changed greatly since this information was published?

EVALUATING WEBSITES

Websites are even more difficult to evaluate. On the Internet, it is possible to create a website that looks and appears credible. Before you assume that a website is an appropriate source for your research, use the same criteria you used for printed materials. Check for accuracy, expert opinions, bias, variety, and currency. Additionally, for these Internet sources, there are a few other points to consider.

THE WEBSITE

What is the main website trying to do? If it is selling something or arguing for or against something, then you may have an issue with bias. Many times, the domain type can give you a clue. Domain types such as *.gov* (for government agencies) and *.edu* (for schools) can be good places to start. For sites that are *.com, .net,* and even *.org,* look at the intentions of the website to decide if there is an ulterior motive other than presenting information.

WHEN TO BEWARE OF SCHOOL WEBSITES

College websites often publish research from their professors, documents that they have on campus, and other great research information. However, many schools also allow students to publish their papers online. This is true of other schools, too—high schools, and even grade schools! Before you use information from a *.edu* website as a source for your research, make sure that the information comes from an authoritative source, not just another student writing a paper like you!

This isn't to say that *.com* websites can't be used. Just make sure that the information passes the tests that you would apply to published sources, and that the website is providing the information for reasons that are appropriate for your research.

CHAPTER 6
THINK STRAIGHT, GET ORGANIZED

You have gathered the information that will be the basis of your paper. It's tempting to start writing now, but you may find that you can't yet present your ideas in the most clear and sensible way. Take the time to get your ideas and information in order, and the time will pay off in a better paper and a higher grade.

NOTE CARD SYSTEM

If you gathered and documented your research on note cards, then you can take that system a step further to organize your paper. The topics you wrote on the top of the cards can also be used to structure your essay. Those headings also show you related information that you can group together, and you can see how all your information might be ordered within the essay.

You first need to go back and organize your cards by topic. Group together all the cards that have the same topic. When you finish, you will have your cards in piles, one topic per pile. You can have any number of piles and any number of cards in each pile. The number of piles of cards and the number of cards in each pile will give you an idea of how long your paper is. Think of each card or two as one section of the paper.

Let's say you are working on a research paper about the history of hula dancing. After completing your research and sorting the cards, your piles might look like this:

Storytelling   7
The hula tells stories about the
ancestors of the Hawaiian people.
                          p. 16

Related to Nature   4
The movements are related to elements in nature, like the swaying
of trees.
                          p. 52

Kahiko   1
The ancient hula has been passed
down for hundreds of years.
                          p. 20

Costumes   3
Hula students are taught how to
make their costumes from plants
and cloth.
                          p. 94

The Banned Dance   2
When the queen converted to
Christianity, she banned public
hula performances.
                          p. 89

The Merrie Monarch   1
His celebration to honor Hawaiian culture is reenacted today.
                          p. 49

The "Hollywood" Hula   8
Dances shown on TV and in movies are usually not authentic.
                          p. 7

Hula Auana   5
The modern version of the hula
is taught in schools alongside the
ancient hula.
                          p. 15

ORDER!

You can save yourself even more time in writing your paper by organizing each pile of topic cards. Lay out the cards for one topic in front of you. Put the ideas and quotes that are related in separate piles together. Then arrange the cards in the order that makes sense. One group of the cards about hula dancing might look like this:

Related to Nature 4 The movements are related to elements in nature, like the swaying of trees. <div align="right">p. 52</div>	Related to Nature 1 "We get our energy from the earth." <div align="right">p. 16</div>
Related to Nature 3 Some hulas retell events such as earthquakes, volcanoes, or storms. <div align="right">p. 105</div>	Related to Nature 6 Drums come from nature— coconut shells, trunks, and stretched fish skins. <div align="right">p. 67</div>
Related to Nature 1 The chants can call out to the clouds for rain, storms, or other kinds of weather. <div align="right">p. 74</div>	Related to Nature 4 Circular movements can stand for the winds or the ocean currents. <div align="right">p. 24</div>
Related to Nature 2 Some traditional hulas use herbs to act out healing someone. <div align="right">p. 80</div>	

Now you can put the stacks of topic cards in the order that you want to write the paper. By doing this, you have the information needed to write the paper in order. Now most of the work in writing is making the connections between one piece of information and another.

The cards in this group, about how hula is related to nature, could be grouped together in a sensible order. There are two cards that talk about movement, so they belong together. There are two cards that talk about how plants are used in the dance, so they can be grouped together. There are also two cards that talk about weather—clouds and storms—so these cards should be grouped together. Once you have made the groups within a group, you can put the cards in the most logical order. The final result looks something like this:

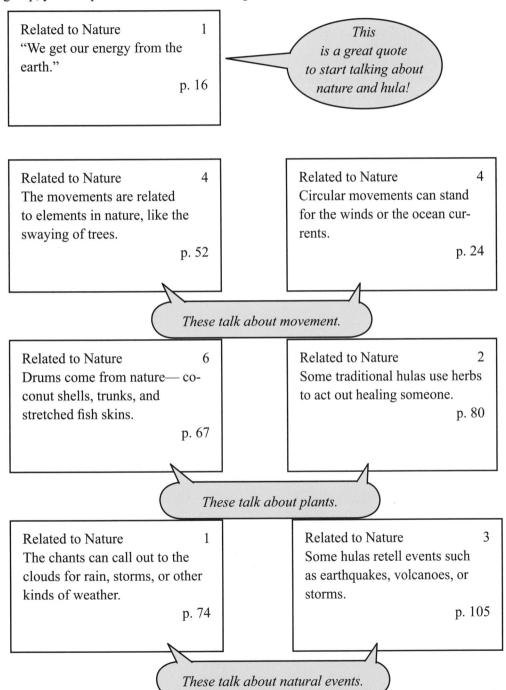

Related to Nature   1
"We get our energy from the earth."
      p. 16

This is a great quote to start talking about nature and hula!

Related to Nature   4
The movements are related to elements in nature, like the swaying of trees.
      p. 52

Related to Nature   4
Circular movements can stand for the winds or the ocean currents.
      p. 24

These talk about movement.

Related to Nature   6
Drums come from nature— coconut shells, trunks, and stretched fish skins.
      p. 67

Related to Nature   2
Some traditional hulas use herbs to act out healing someone.
      p. 80

These talk about plants.

Related to Nature   1
The chants can call out to the clouds for rain, storms, or other kinds of weather.
      p. 74

Related to Nature   3
Some hulas retell events such as earthquakes, volcanoes, or storms.
      p. 105

These talk about natural events.

Compare this arrangement of cards to how they were first presented. The information is the same, but the first group of cards was a bit of a mess! The information was all there, but it was not presented in a way that made a strong statement. Now, the cards show some organization. Using this organized group of cards, you would have a much easier time writing a paper that showed a connection and logical flow of ideas.

BRANCH OUT—TRY USING A TREE!

Trees are a way to show the logic behind the information in your paper. You can make a tree with note cards, you can build it with self-stick notes, or you can draw it on a large sheet of paper. Trees are great organization tools. The only drawback is that they can take up a lot of room.

When you make a tree, you start with the thesis, or topic statement. Then show the ideas that you are including to defend your thesis. Then, next to each idea, you will show your supporting details. These details are those pieces of information you found in your research.

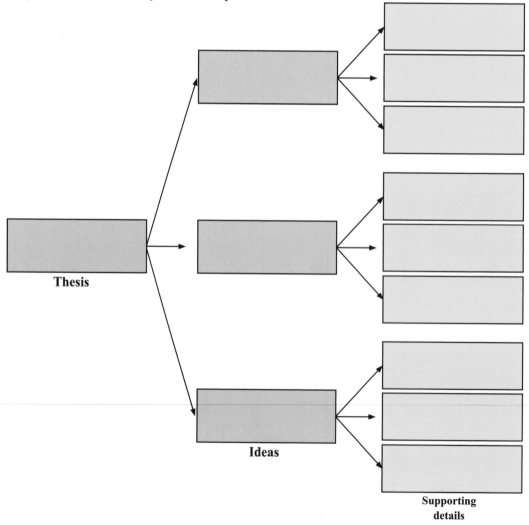

Thesis

Ideas

Supporting details

So you could take the same note cards from the hula research and create a tree. This only covers part of the information, but it is enough to give you the idea.

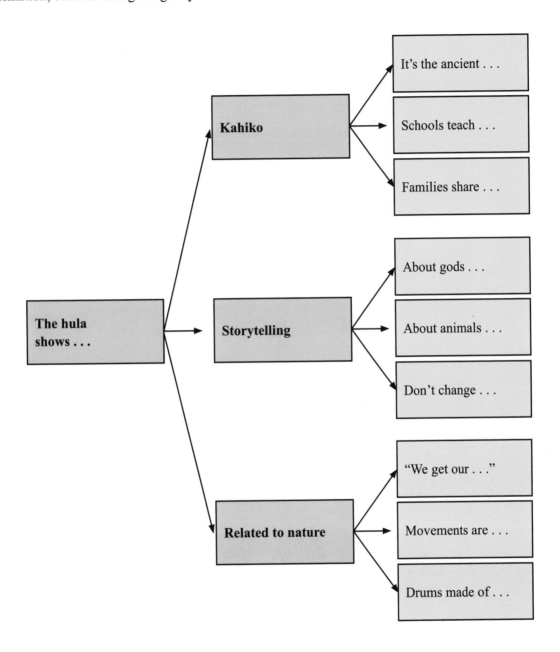

If you use a tree to organize your ideas, use this checklist to be sure that your ideas are organized properly:

Tree Checklist

- ☐ All of the branches tell something about the thesis.
- ☐ Each idea has at least two supporting details.
- ☐ Each part of the tree is a complete thought or sentence.
- ☐ Ideas don't repeat from one branch to another.

THE OLD-FASHIONED OUTLINE

You have probably written outlines for classes. They are good study aids. Outlines have a very clear structure and are easy to read. For planning a paper, outlines are terrific. They show the information that you have. They also show in what order you will present the information in your paper. Outlines can also show information you have that does not support the thesis so you know what *not* to use in the paper.

Your teacher might require that you turn in an outline before your paper is due. This is pretty common, especially for your first paper for a teacher. This allows him or her to check your ideas and offer suggestions. Your teacher might suggest that you add information or even scale back. This is very common. Don't take it personally if you have to go back and revise or do a bit more research. It's better to make the changes early so that you write a better paper later.

Most word-processing software has a tool that will help you create an outline. You can use the software to do the numbering for you. Then if you want to change the order of items in your outline, a simple "drag and drop" will do. The outline feature will automatically renumber for you.

Using a word-processing program also makes it easier to keep up with the different versions of your outlines. If a new version of the outline doesn't work as well as an older one, you can simply go back to the older file.

In an outline, you will write common ideas under general headings and arrange your ideas so you can see how they relate to each other. For example, in a paper that will be written in sequential order, the outline topics should also appear in sequence. If you are writing a compare-and-contrast paper, each idea should show how your subjects are alike or different. You would put all similarities together in the outline and put all differences in another part of the outline, rather than go back and forth.

The numbering system for outlines is pretty much the same for any teacher, unless they give you specific directions otherwise. It would look like this:

I. (Roman numeral with a period)
    A. (Uppercase letter with a period)
        1. (Arabic or counting number with a period)
            a. (Lowercase letter with a period)
                (1) (Arabic or counting number with parentheses)
                    (a) (Lowercase letter with parentheses)
                (2)
            b.
        2.
    B.
II.

The logic in an outline tells you that if you list an *A,* you have to at least list a *B.* For every *1,* there must be a *2.* Think of it this way: If you were giving your mom reasons why you should be able to go to the mall, you wouldn't say, "First, I need new clothes," then never give a second reason. It's the same with outlines. For each level you start with a *I, A, 1, a,* and so on, you have to give at least one other piece of information at the same level. Without it, your argument would be weak. Either get rid of that point or find more information to support your idea.

A ROMAN NUMERAL REFRESHER

It would be nice if all outlines had only three main points, then you would only need to use I, II, and III. But that would be a very short paper! So here's a quick reminder of the Roman numerals through 15, just in case you want to write a nice, long paper.

I	1	VI	6	XI	11
II	2	VII	7	XII	12
III	3	VIII	8	XIII	13
IV	4	IX	9	XIV	14
V	5	X	10	XV	15

Here is an example of the beginning of the outline for the history of the hula. Since this tells about a historical topic, it is written in sequential order. To help keep focus, notice that we write the thesis at the beginning of the outline:

Thesis: The hula dance shows the culture and history of the Hawaiian people.

I.   The hula is a form of storytelling.
    A. Hula is a way of retelling the stories of the ancestors.
        1. Some hulas tell of the creation of Hawaii when Kilauea erupted.
        2. Some hulas are done to celebrate certain gods or certain phases of the Moon.
    B. Hula tells about the beliefs of ancient Hawaiians.
        1. A hula can explain how people communicated with the gods to ask for help or favors.
        2. The dance shows how the Hawaiians believed they had qualities like the gods.

Everything you write should back up your thesis.

Every entry in an outline should be one sentence.

You don't have to use every level of an outline. We don't go past the Arabic number in this part of the outline.

Every time you move to a more detailed level on the outline, you indent. When you move to a more general level, move left again.

C. Hula passes along ancient Hawaiian history.

  1. One hula tells the story of the birth of King Kamehameha.

  2. Another dance tells the story of a battle between Hawaiians and people from another part of the Pacific islands.

  3. Another hula tells of what the land on the Hawaiian islands used to look like before modern civilization.

II. The hula shows the Hawaiians' relationship with nature.

  . . . and so on.

All Roman numerals line up on the left. All uppercase letters line up on the left, and so on.

Every indented level should back up, or support, the sentence in the level that it's under.

No matter what type of paper you are writing, the outline structure is the same. For example, your thesis may classify the different types of hulas rather than tell its history. In that case, each Roman numeral would describe one type of hula:

Thesis: The different types of hula serve different roles in the Hawaiian society.

I. The first type of hula is the hula `âla`apapa.

  A. This dance is a dramatic . . .

    1. It uses . . .

    2. Dancers move . . .

  B. Musicians use . . .

    1. Instruments . . .

    2. Chanters . . .

II. The second type of hula is the hula `auana.

  A. This dance is an informal . . .

    1. There is no . . .

    2. Dancers wear . . .

  B. Music is . . .

    1. Drummers will . . .

    2. Singers . . .

    . . .and so on.

If your thesis is an argument that the hula is a religious ceremony and not just a dance, you would write an outline with your reasons. Each reason would be a Roman numeral. You would work up to ending with your strongest argument.

Maybe your thesis explains how European exploration caused the decline of hula as a traditional Hawaiian dance. Your outline might have different types of European explorers, such as James Cook and Christian missionaries, as each Roman numeral. The details under each Roman numeral would tell about the explorers and how they impacted the tradition of the hula.

What if your thesis was to compare the Hawaiian hula with the Whirling Dervish of Turkey? (Yes, that's a real dance!) Your outline could have one Roman numeral for each dance, with a lot of details under each dance. Another choice would be to list each way the two dances are similar as a Roman numeral, and talk in detail about that common aspect for the letters and numbers in the outline.

If you use an outline to organize your ideas, use this checklist to make sure your outline is complete:

Outline Checklist

☐   Thesis is included at the beginning of the outline.

☐   Each outline entry has one sentence.

☐   Outline is indented and numbered/lettered properly.

☐   Each level of outline has at least two entries every time it is used.

CHAPTER 7
GETTING PENCIL TO PAPER

You've prepared for this moment, and the time has come! It's time to start writing. With other writing projects, you may have suffered a bit of writer's block—not knowing what to write and not being able to start. Now, because you took the time to research and create an outline, tree, or detailed note cards, you have all the information you need to get started.

KNOW YOUR AUDIENCE

Before you start writing, you need to think a bit about your audience, or for whom you are writing. If you write with only your teacher in mind as your reader, you may not say enough. You know your teacher, and he or she probably knows a bit about the topic you chose. If you write your paper thinking that your teacher already knows about your topic, you may not give enough information to develop your paper properly.

In other words, don't assume that your audience is a teacher or an expert on your topic. You will be more likely to explain your points more clearly and include enough detail to make your points strong and clear.

INTRODUCING . . . YOUR PAPER!

Your introduction is the first paragraph of your research paper. The job of an introduction is to get your reader's attention. It generates interest in your topic. It also gives your reader your thesis.

WHEN DOES THE INTRODUCTION NOT COME FIRST?

Some writers find that the introduction is the hardest part of the paper to write. The beauty of the introduction is that you *don't* have to write it first. As a matter of fact, you may find that you write a better introduction after you write the body of the paper because you will be able to focus clearly on the information coming in the paper. So you can choose to write the introduction first; write the introduction after you write the body of the paper; or write a rough version of the introduction first, write the rest of the paper, and then go back and refine the introduction.

When it comes to writing an introduction, there really is no one correct way. You just have to find what works best for you.

You have some flexibility in starting your introduction. The key is to start in a way that makes the reader want to find out more. You could start with an unusual fact related to your thesis, give an interesting quotation, state an important statistic, or even ask a question. We will give you a few examples in a moment to see how these work.

The next part of the introduction should be a few sentences that give a little background about the sentence with which you started. These sentences should also start leading the reader to the thesis for the entire paper.

Think of your introduction this way:

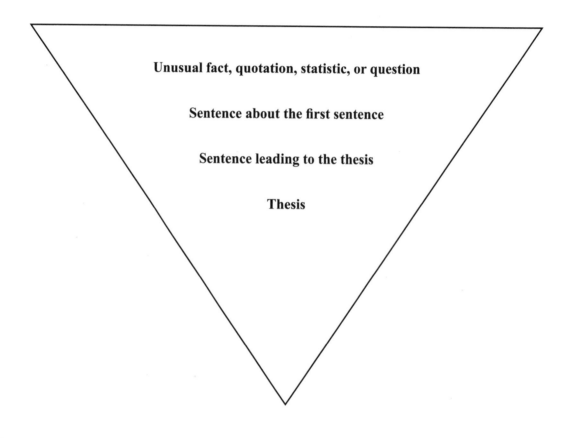

Unusual fact, quotation, statistic, or question

Sentence about the first sentence

Sentence leading to the thesis

Thesis

So let's say you are writing a research paper on the use of the spitball in Major League Baseball. Here are a few ways you could start your paper:

Unusual Fact

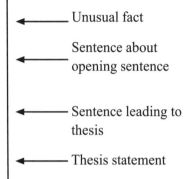

Because spitballs move so unpredictably, they are very difficult for hitters to see. A spitball is simply a pitch where the pitcher uses spit or another substance to change the way the ball moves when it is thrown. It was used by many pitchers in the early 1900s, was banned in 1920, and is possibly still used today. The spitball represents an important, but often under-recognized, tradition in baseball.

— Unusual fact

— Sentence about opening sentence

— Sentence leading to thesis

— Thesis statement

Interesting Quotation

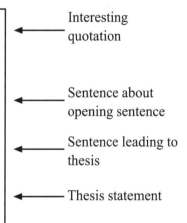

Hall of Fame pitcher Bob Gibson said, "Rules or no rules, pitchers are going to throw spitters. It's a matter of survival." A spitter, or spitball, is simply a pitch where the pitcher uses spit or another substance to change the way the ball moves when it is thrown. It was used by many pitchers in the early 1900s, was banned in 1920, and is possibly still used today. The spitball represents an important, but often under-recognized, tradition in baseball.

Interesting quotation

Sentence about opening sentence

Sentence leading to thesis

Thesis statement

Important Statistic

> When the spitball was a legal pitch in Major League Baseball, pitchers were able to win up to 40 games a season—an amount that is nearly impossible now. A spitball is simply a pitch where the pitcher uses spit or another substance to change the way the ball moves when it is thrown. It was used by many pitchers in the early 1900s, was banned in 1920, and is possibly still used today. The spitball represents an important, but often under-recognized, tradition in baseball.

◄— Important statistic

◄— Sentence about opening sentence

◄— Sentence leading to thesis

◄— Thesis statement

Question

> Have you ever wondered why the spitball is banned from baseball? A spitball is simply a pitch where the pitcher uses spit or another substance to change the way the ball moves when it is thrown. It was used by many pitchers in the early 1900s, was banned in 1920, and is possibly still used today. The spitball represents an important, but often under-recognized, tradition in baseball.

◄— Question

◄— Sentence about opening sentence

◄— Sentence leading to thesis

◄— Thesis statement

With these examples, you can see that there are a few ways to start an introduction, but the farther into the paragraph you go, the information is the same. In each case, you get the reader's attention, talk about the opening sentence, move toward the thesis, and then state the thesis. This may take more than four sentences, but as a rule, it should not be less than four sentences long.

THE MEAT AND POTATOES OF YOUR PAPER

The body of your paper is all of the paragraphs that you write to explain or prove your thesis. The body will have many paragraphs. Exactly how many depends on your assignment and the research you have done.

Each paragraph should follow a similar pattern. You start with a topic sentence. Then you give examples and facts to support the topic of the paragraph. Finally, explain how the information relates to the thesis. Following this pattern will help you make your information clear and show the reader the connection between the research and the thesis you chose.

ABOUT THOSE EXAMPLES. . .

The information you gathered in your research will become the examples that you use to support your thesis. You can either include those research points as a paraphrase of what you found, a summary of what you found, or a direct quotation from the source. These examples should not come from you, as you are not a recognized authority. The explanation that comes after these examples lets you make connections and tell how the research you use supports your thesis. In other words, let the experts give the information in your paragraphs. Then use the last few sentences in each paragraph to put your "spin" on the information.

Another note about direct quotes: Don't use too many of them. You should choose quotations when they are said so well that you would change the meaning or the tone by rewording them. When you do use a direct quote, you should spend at least twice as much room on your paper explaining the quote and connecting it to your thesis. This shows that you understand the link between the research and your thesis.

WHAT'S THE DIFFERENCE?

If you don't use a direct quotation, you have the choice between summarizing and paraphrasing. What is the difference between the two? A summary shortens information to just the main idea of the material. A paraphrase is saying the same idea in a different way. A summary says *less*. A paraphrase says the same amount, just differently.

A final note about direct quotes: Don't drop them into your writing like a bomb. They need to be included in your writing in a subtle way.

Look at this example that highlights poor use of a quotation:

Poor Use of Quotation:

George Hildebrand was probably the first umpire in the major leagues to recognize this new, questionable pitch. "One day I was warming up with a young pitcher named Frank Corridon. I notice him throwing a slow ball with quite a break. He did this by wetting the tips of his fingers before pitching."

There is nothing to lead the reader into the quote. It's a bomb!

Blending quotations into your writing is not very difficult. Just take the time to add a few words to introduce the quote. This example shows how the same quote can be introduced into the text in a way that transitions nicely:

Good Use of Quotation:

George Hildebrand was probably the first player in the major leagues to teach this new, questionable pitch. In a letter to a baseball statistician, he said, "One day I was warming up with a young pitcher named Frank Corridon. I notice him throwing a slow ball with quite a break. He did this by wetting the tips of his fingers before pitching."

This phrase makes the quotation blend into the rest of the paragraph.

THE QUALITIES OF GOOD PARAGRAPHS

Since these paragraphs are the "meat and potatoes" of your paper, it is important that you think about how they are written. There are four traits that make good paragraphs: focus, development, clarity, and technique. Let's look at each trait and examples that illustrate how important they are.

FOCUS

Focus is what keeps you from going off-topic. Each paragraph should address only one idea—the idea given in the topic sentence. Here is an example:

Lack of Focus:

Spitballs became an important part of a pitcher's arsenal in the early 1900s. Pitcher Elmer Stricklett was one of the first known pitchers to use the spitball in the majors. He used the pitch when he threw for the Chicago White Sox, starting in 1904. Stricklett was not part of the Chicago Black Sox team that was steeped in scandal a few years later.

◄—— Topic sentence

◄—— This doesn't have anything to do with the topic sentence!

Good Focus:

Spitballs became an important part of a pitcher's arsenal in the early 1900s. Pitcher Elmer Stricklett was one of the first known pitchers to use the spitball in the majors. He used the pitch when he threw for the Chicago White Sox, starting in 1904. He went on to pitch for the Brooklyn Dodgers. As he mastered the spitball, his Earned Run Average went from a sad 10.29 to a very respectable 2.27. Hitters had a very hard time making contact with this new, tricky pitch.

◄—— Topic sentence

◄—— This paragraph has focus throughout.

DEVELOPMENT

Each paragraph should give the reader enough information to fully understand the topic sentence. Good development is a balance between giving enough information to be clear, and not too much to be boring. Here is an example:

Poor Development:

The rules about spitballs were not exactly clear. The 1890 rule book explained that discoloring or damaging the ball was against the rules.

— Topic sentence

— There isn't enough information to explain the topic sentence.

Too Much Development:

The rules about spitballs were not exactly clear. The 1890 rule book explained that discoloring or damaging the ball was against the rules. The question was whether or not spit, or saliva, fell into the category of discoloring or damaging the ball. Since spit is usually clear, it may well not discolor the ball. There were no limitations on players getting sweat on the ball, since that could happen in the normal course of play. So a little sweat was okay, but was a little spit okay? There certainly wasn't a way to measure how much spit was too much.

— Topic sentence

This just goes on too long!

Good Development:

The rules about spitballs were not exactly clear. The 1890 rule book explained that discoloring or damaging the ball was against the rules. The question was whether or not spit, or saliva, fell into the category of discoloring or damaging the ball. The rule book had not accounted for this method of "doctoring" the ball.

—— Topic sentence

This describes the topic sentence well.

CLARITY

Your thoughts as a writer should be perfectly clear to the reader. You want to be sure that the reader knows exactly what you mean. This comes from choosing clear, concise words, and writing enough of them. Here is an example:

Poor Clarity:

Pitchers used spit on their pitches in two basic ways. Pitchers could use spit on one part of the ball to make it break. They could also use spit while they threw a splitter. These pitches were hard for the batters to see. Batters would look to one part of the plate when the ball came to another. Maybe they looked left when the ball went right.

—— Topic sentence

—— Unless you know about baseball, this is very unclear. What is breaking? What is a splitter?

—— This is the opposite of concise. The writer uses two sentences to say essentially the same thing.

TECHNIQUE

The technique you use in writing is twofold. First, you should choose words that are vivid and engaging. The writing should use as little passive voice as possible. The second part of technique is how well you design your sentences. Interesting reading has sentences that have different structures and length. Here is an example:

WHAT IS PASSIVE VOICE? (EXACTLY!)

See if you get the joke after you read the answer to the question.

Passive voice describes sentences that use a form of the verb *to be*. For example: *be, is, are, were,* and *was* are all forms of the verb *to be*. These sentences are not as exciting to read as sentences that use active verbs. See for yourself:

Passive Voice	Active Voice
The sky is blue.	The sky appears blue.
We were tired.	We felt tired.
The game is over.	The game ended.
I could be convinced.	Convince me.
	Now do you get the joke? (Hint: Read the title of this section until you do!)

Poor Technique: Many famous pitchers were spitball throwers. Many pitchers were able to pitch longer because they threw the spitball. Pitchers were able to avoid injury by throwing spitballs.	These sentences start the same way, and are similar in length. Boring! Notice all of the passive sentences?
Good Technique: Many famous pitchers threw spitballs. Because the spitball caused fewer arm injuries, these pitchers extended their careers by years. The spitballs let older and injury-prone pitchers become winning hurlers again.	These sentences vary in length and structure. They are more interesting to read. These active verbs make the reading more exciting.

IN CONCLUSION. . .

Once you have taken all the time needed to write the body of your research paper, you may find it hard to write the conclusion. Writers often feel like they have already said everything there is to say. Good writers know that the conclusion is the most important part of the paper, because it is likely to be what the reader remembers the best.

Conclusions restate the thesis. This lets you as the writer show the reader that you have done your job in proving your thesis. The thesis can be worded a little differently, but the reader should recognize it as the point you stated in your introduction.

Conclusions also emphasize your strongest arguments or ideas. You don't have to repeat your ideas from the body of the paper. Instead, use different words to "connect the dots" one last time for your reader.

Finally, conclusions give readers something to think about. This could be applying your ideas in a way that the reader can relate to, or providing specifics on how your thesis statement is still important today.

The one thing you should *not* include in the conclusion is any new information that was not included in the rest of your research paper. Do not add new quotations or facts here. You have the body of the paper to introduce all of your evidence and information. You will lose points on your paper if you drop in something here that you have not mentioned before.

The conclusion looks a lot like the *opposite* of the introduction. Where the introduction looks like an upside-down triangle, the conclusion looks more like this:

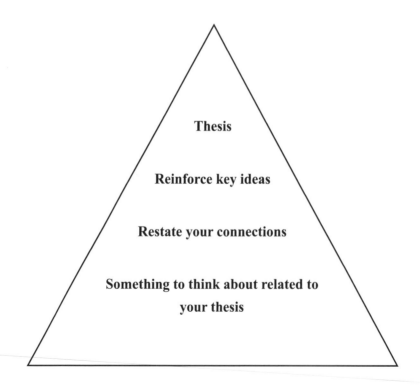

> The spitball characterizes a tradition in baseball of which many fans are not aware. Spitballs were the trademark pitch of dozens of great pitchers over the last 100 years. The pitch also gave batters a challenge in an era when batters were able to improve their statistics by stealing signs, improving their equipment, and building stronger bodies. History may well show that the spitball brought a challenge back to the game that seems to be missing today.

← Thesis

← Present your strongest arguments.

← The answer to "So what?"

WRITING A TITLE

Unless you had a brainstorm somewhere along the line, you probably still need a title for your paper. Now you should be able to think of one.

Your title should be specific. Don't give a research paper a clever title unless it also happens to tell what the paper is really about.

Weak Title	Strong Title
Women in Basketball	The History of the WNBA
Not as Simple as It Seems	Understanding Alice in Wonderland: Not as Simple as It Seems

In addition to being specific, use these guidelines for writing your title:

- Titles are *not* complete sentences.
- Only underline or put quotation marks around titles of other works in your title. Don't underline *your* title.
- Capitalize all major words in the title, including the first and last words in your title.
- Don't capitalize an article like *a, an,* or *the* unless it is the first word of the title.
- Do not capitalize short prepositions like *of, on, to,* or *in.*
- Do not capitalize the conjunctions *and, but,* and *or.*
- Do capitalize other conjunctions like *when, although,* and *while.*

CHAPTER 8
GIVE CREDIT WHERE CREDIT IS DUE

In the previous chapter, we briefly talked about summarizing, paraphrasing, and quoting your sources. It is important to know how to incorporate each into your paper, but it is also important to know *why*.

PLAGIARISM

Merriam-Webster defines plagiarism as "to steal and pass off (the ideas or words of another) as one's own: use (another's production) without crediting the source; to commit literary theft: present as new and original an idea or product derived from an existing source."

You can be accused of plagiarism if you change a few words instead of most of the words in someone else's writing. For example, take a passage that says, "The Republic of Singapore is an island city-state and is the smallest country in Southeast Asia." Then say that you write, as a paraphrase, "The island city-state Republic of Singapore is the smallest country in Southeast Asia." This is still considered plagiarism. The words and ideas are so similar that you might as well have said the original statement to begin with.

It is also plagiarism if you summarize correctly but don't give credit to the author in footnotes, endnotes, or the bibliography. Even though you may have rewritten ideas and information using your own words, the ideas you used to create the new sentence are not yours. You must take the time to give credit to your sources.

To avoid plagiarism, you must credit your sources whenever you use:

- another person's idea or opinion
- any facts, statistics, graphs, or drawings that are not common knowledge
- a person's actual spoken or written word
- a paraphrase of a person's spoken or written words

WHAT IS COMMON KNOWLEDGE?

You do not have to credit information that is common knowledge. The trick is, then, to recognize information that is common knowledge.

Common knowledge is information that most people know. The fact that George W. Bush was elected president in 2000 is common knowledge. The value of *pi* is common knowledge. Although this information could be found in an encyclopedia, this type of information is common knowledge and would not need to be cited.

FOOTNOTES AND ENDNOTES

Footnotes and endnotes give credit to the writer whose words or ideas you used in your paper. A footnote is a note at the bottom of the page that tells where your information came from. Endnotes give the same information, but they are listed at the very end of the paper rather than on the pages that the information appears.

Direct quotations, images, and statistics must have a footnote or endnote. The ideas that you summarize and paraphrase do not require footnotes or endnotes. For these, you will simply include the sources in the bibliography, which is covered in Chapter 9.

Check your assignment to see if your teacher has been specific about asking for either endnotes or footnotes. If your teacher doesn't specify, then you can choose.

So which is better? It depends. It is easier to read footnotes than endnotes, because you don't have to flip from information early in the paper to the notes at the end of the paper. Each note appears on the same page that the information appears. Footnotes are fairly easy to include if you are writing your final paper on a computer, as word processor programs can place them on the page and make them fit nicely. It is hard to know exactly how much room to leave at the bottom of each page for the footnote information. If you don't leave enough room, you run the risk of having to rewrite or retype that page. If you are hand writing or typing your paper on a typewriter, then endnotes will be much easier for you. Endnotes go on a separate page (or pages) at the end of your paper, before your bibliography.

STYLE IS EVERYTHING

There are a number of styles that you can use to write endnotes and footnotes. There is MLA, APA, the Chicago Style, CSE, and more. Which style you use is completely up to your teacher. He or she may even have a different style that you should use. Check your assignment or ask your teacher if you are unsure. Since the MLA style is most common, that is what will be discussed in this book.

The *Modern Language Association (MLA)* style is the most commonly used in high schools and college classes in areas such as literature, languages, and the arts. The *American Psychological Association (APA)* is used most often for college-level papers in the areas of psychology and education. *The Chicago Manual of Style* is a book that is used by publishers for the proper way to write articles, papers, and more. The style book describes its own type of footnotes and endnotes. The *Council of Science Editors (CSE)*, formerly known as the *Council of Biology Editors (CBE)*, style is most common for college-level papers in the science fields.

WHERE DO I FIND THE INFORMATION?

When citing information from your research, you'll need to know where to look to find the information you'll need from each source. Books, articles, websites, etc., are each cited in a different way. Check further into this chapter to find out what specific information you'll need to cite all different types of sources.

BOOKS (INCLUDING ENCYCLOPEDIAS)

All of the information you need for the footnotes and endnotes you write are on the title page and the next page, which contains the copyright information. If there is more than one date listed for the copyright, use the most recent one.

MAGAZINES, NEWSPAPERS, AND OTHER PERIODICALS

Periodicals take a bit more work to find the information. The title of the periodical and date are usually on the cover. The publisher and location are found somewhere on the first few pages, usually around the table of contents. The author, if one is listed, is printed on the page with the article.

GOVERNMENT DOCUMENTS

Government documents are published like books and periodicals (depending on the size). Refer to those sections to help find your information.

FILM, AUDIO, OR TV

If you have packaging (like the box for a DVD or cassette tape), look on and inside it for the information you need. If you watched a TV show, for example, look at the credits at the beginning and end of the show to find the names and dates you need. When all else fails, there are websites such as the Internet Movie Database (http://www.imdb.com). These will have information about television programs and movies that will help you document this type of source.

COMPUTER SOFTWARE

Software has information on the packaging, sometimes in small prints on the sides of the package. You can nearly always find the information you need in the program itself if it has a "Help. . . About. . ." menu.

THE INTERNET

Internet sites are usually the most difficult to find information for. There is no standard way to document the site, so look thoroughly throughout the page you are using. If there is not enough information there, then go to the home page of the website and look for the missing details there. Remember that if you cannot find pertinent information about a website, you may not be using a reputable site.

START WRITING NOTES!

The words that need footnotes or endnotes are followed with a small number that is written slightly above a line like this: [1]. (The high, small formatting is called superscript, by the way.) This is the same whether you are going to use footnotes or endnotes. So if you are using a direct quotation, you would mark it like this: "The Republic of Singapore is an island city-state and is the smallest country in Southeast Asia."[1] The next information that needs an endnote or footnote would be numbered with a [2], then next with a [3], and so on. The numbers will continue through the paper—don't start numbering at [1] again on a new page.

Each number will correspond to the footnote or endnote that tells the source information. So, for example, if you were going to write a footnote or endnote for the quote about Singapore above, it would be numbered with a superscript [1] as well. It would look like this:

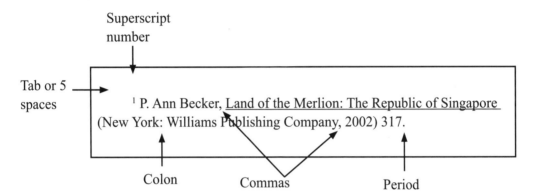

Superscript number

Tab or 5 spaces

[1] P. Ann Becker, <u>Land of the Merlion: The Republic of Singapore</u> (New York: Williams Publishing Company, 2002) 317.

Colon   Commas   Period

Each type of source has a slightly different footnote or endnote entry; much of the rest of this chapter will focus on specific examples so you can see how to note websites, radio shows, journals, books, and more. Before you skim that information, however, there are a few more things to know.

Unlike in a bibliography, the author's name is always written as it appears on the published material. Don't include titles like Mr., Dr., and PhD. that you might see on the cover or title page of the book. *Do* include Jr., Sr., I, II, III, etc., because these are considered part of the name.

If the city where the book was published is not a major city, then include the state or country as well. If more than one city is listed, use only the first one in your citation. If you are citing a publication like a large national magazine or newspaper, there is no need to list the city.

If you have two or more notes from the same source, use the author's last name and the relevant page number for the footnote or endnote. If another entry in the Singapore paper came from the same book as we just noted, the footnote or endnote would look like this:

[2] Becker, 319–320.

Finally, your footnote or endnote should read like a sentence. It has only one period. When you read about bibliographies, you will see that they use multiple periods. Since footnotes and endnotes give source information and so does a bibliography, don't confuse how to write the two. They are very different.

The rest of this chapter is devoted to specific examples of footnotes and endnotes for different kinds of sources. Don't spend time reading each entry in detail. Instead, just skim it to find the type of footnotes or endnotes you need. You can copy the way the note is written with your own sources.

BOOKS

Book with one author:

[1] Bob Brinker, The Story of Singapore (Toronto: Asian Press, 2002) 125–26.

Book with one editor:

[2] John Greene, ed., Singapore Heat (Los Angeles: Smith Publishing, 1994) 12–13.

Book with two authors:

[3] Richard Dart and Michelle Nolan, Singapore (Singapore: Binding Press, 2004) 261–63.

Book with two editors:

[4] Andrea Chen and K.M. Granada, eds., The Merlion's Shadow (Hong Kong: Second Chance Publishing, 1996) 241.

Book with three or more authors:

[5] Jacques Caan, et al., The Politics of Southeast Asia (San Francisco: Heath Inc., 1998) 45.

Book with three or more editors:

[6] Manny Landis, et al., eds., The Birth of the Singapore Nation (New York: Melvin's Press, 1995) 162–66.

Book with no author or editor given:

[7] The 2005 Guide to Singapore (New York: Charles Publishing Group, 2005) 79.

Book that has been translated:

[8] Lee Kuan Yew, The Autobiography of Lee Kuan Yew, trans. M.E. Heller (Chicago: Bandera, 1999) 107.

ENCYCLOPEDIAS AND OTHER REFERENCE BOOKS

Article from an encyclopedia with no author given:

[9] "Singapore," Encyclopedia of Southeast Asia, 1998 ed.

Article from an encyclopedia with one author:

[10] Landry B. Preston, "Singapore: History," <u>New World Encyclopedia</u>, 2002 ed. (New York: New World Publishing, 2001) 294.

ARTICLES FROM MAGAZINES, JOURNALS, NEWSPAPERS, ETC.

Article from a magazine, journal, or newspaper with no author given:

[11] "Uncovering Singapore's Past," <u>Montreal Globe and News</u> 16 Nov. 2004: B12.

[12] "Singapore Grows Up," <u>Business Weekly</u> 7 Feb. 2003: 22–24.

Article from a magazine, journal, or newspaper with one or more authors:

[13] James Crawford, "The Fall of Singapore," <u>Straits News</u> [Singapore] 21 Jan. 2005: 5.

[14] Jeannette Yeo and Lee Goh, "The Future of Singapore," <u>This Week in News</u> 9 Jan. 2003: 72.

Review of book, movie, film, or product:

[15] Harry Poh, rev. of <u>Singapore: History and Geography</u>, CD-ROM, Harris Technology, <u>Computer Magazine</u> Aug. 1999: 19.

[16] Katherine Nguyen, "The Singapore Way," rev. of <u>Singapore: The Movie</u>, dir. Marcus James, <u>National Review</u> [Singapore] 11 Nov. 2001: C6.

GOVERNMENT DOCUMENT

[17] Singapore, Minister of Economic Affairs, <u>Singapore's Economic Outlook: May 2004</u> (Singapore: Minister of Economic Affairs, 2004) 11–12.

[18] United States, National Council on American-Asian Affairs, <u>Promoting United States-Singapore Relations</u> (Washington: GPO, 2001) 8.

INTERVIEW

[19] Helstrom Long, personal interview, 21 July 2006.

FILM, AUDIO, OR TV

Film or video recording:

[20] <u>The Singapore Story</u>, dir. Amy Shaw, perf. Vince Tan, DVD, HBO, 2005.

[21] <u>A Simple Life</u>, dir. Nick Yan, writ. Jim Son, perf. Mort Smith and Ming Won, VHS, Universe, 1999.

Audio recording:

[22] Alex Yan, <u>Curry and Ginger</u>, Tokyo, Audioworks, 1996.

Television or radio:

[23] <u>Lance Kwan Live</u>, SNews, Singapore, 27 May 2004.

[24] <u>Lee Kuan Yew Speaks</u>, WSON, Houston, 6 Oct. 2002.

COMPUTER SOFTWARE

[25] <u>Singapore: A Multimedia Tour</u>, CD-ROM (Los Angeles: PCTools, 1998).

INTERNET

[26] "Singapore: A Brief History," <u>Historic Information Services</u>, May 2000, 9 Apr. 2006 <http://www.his.org /sing2000.html>.

INTERNET DATES

For Internet sites, you will often use two dates in your footnote or endnote. If the website tells the copyright date, then you need to include that in the note. (Look at the very bottom of the web page.) You should also include the date that you accessed the information on the website. The copyright date is first. The date you accessed the information is second.

CHAPTER 9
PLEASE NAME YOUR SOURCES

Your bibliography is a list of the magazines, books, newspapers, and other sources that you used to complete your research. The bibliography is placed at the end of your paper, starting on a new sheet of paper titled "Bibliography."

The bibliography is the second step in crediting your research sources. Your footnotes or endnotes gave credit for direct quotes, statistics, facts, and the like. However, you also used your research sources for information that you summarized and paraphrased. The bibliography credits *all* of your sources instead of those that you used more directly. Bibliographies are also handy if a reader wants to find out more information about your research topic. A reader can find the books, magazines, websites, etc., to do further reading on his or her own.

STYLE COUNTS HERE, TOO!

Just like with footnotes and endnotes, bibliographies can be written in MLA style, APA style, Chicago style, CBE style, and more. And just as with endnotes and footnotes, be sure you check your assignment or ask your teacher to know exactly what style you are expected to use. Also as with the endnotes and footnotes, since MLA style is so commonly used, that's the style that we will focus on here.

From the previous chapter, you know that the endnotes and footnotes were numbered and were listed in the order that they appeared in the research paper. This is *not* the case with bibliographies. Instead, bibliographies are not numbered. They are listed in order of the author's last name. (This also means that sources without an author listed come first, in order of the title of the source.)

The formatting of bibliography entries is different from endnotes and footnotes, too. Remember, only the first line of endnotes and footnotes is indented by inserting a tab. With bibliographies, you do the opposite. The first line is typed starting at the left side of the page without an indent. Any additional lines for the entry are indented from the left. If you are typing the paper on a typewriter, this is done with five spaces. On a computer, look to see how to make a "hanging indent." If you are writing the paper by hand, then just indent the lines about a half-inch. (If the bibliography entry is short enough to fit on one line, then don't worry about any indentation for that source.)

Another big change from endnotes and footnotes is that, even if you use a source more than once in the paper, you only list it once in the bibliography.

WHERE TO FIND THE INFORMATION

You will find information for bibliographies in the same places you looked for footnotes and endnotes. Refer to Chapter 8 if you need a reminder.

READY, SET, CITE!

For the bibliography entries, we will use the same sources as from the previous chapter on endnotes and footnotes. This will let you compare them if you need to see the difference between footnotes/endnotes and bibliography entries for any particular type of source.

Here is an example of a basic bibliography entry:

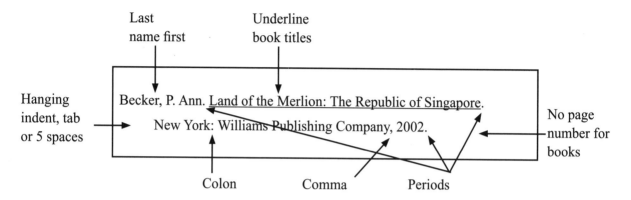

The rest of the information regarding bibliography sources is the same as the information you learned in the previous chapter. This will help you determine what to include in the author's name, how to write the city, and so on.

Finally, just like in Chapter 8, the rest of this chapter is devoted to specific examples of bibliographies for different kinds of sources. As before, don't spend time reading each entry in detail. Skim it to find the type of bibliography entries you need. You can copy the way the note is written and add your own sources.

BOOKS

Book with one author:

Brinker, Bob. The Story of Singapore. Toronto: Asian Press, 2002.

Book with one editor:

Greene, John, ed. Singapore Heat. Los Angeles: Smith Publishing, 1994.

Book with two authors:

Dart, Richard, and Michelle Nolan. Singapore. Singapore: Binding Press, 2004.

Book with two editors:

Chen, Andrea, and K.M. Granada, eds. The Merlion's Shadow. Hong Kong: Second Chance Publishing, 1996.

Book with three or more authors:

Caan, Jacques, et al. <u>The Politics of Southeast Asia</u>. San Francisco: Heath Inc., 1998.

Book with three or more editors:

Landis, Manny, et al., eds. <u>The Birth of the Singapore Nation</u>. New York: Melvin's Press, 1995.

Book with no author or editor given:

<u>The 2005 Guide to Singapore</u>. New York: Charles Publishing Group, 2005.

Book that has been translated:

Yew, Lee Kuan. <u>The Autobiography of Lee Kuan Yew</u>. Trans. M.E. Heller. Chicago: Bandera, 1999.

ENCYCLOPEDIAS AND OTHER REFERENCE BOOKS

Article from an encyclopedia with no author given:

"Singapore." <u>Encyclopedia of Southeast Asia</u>. 1998 ed. Boston: Freedom Press, 1997.

Article from an encyclopedia with one author:

Preston, Landry B. "Singapore: History." <u>New World Encyclopedia</u>. 2002 ed. New York: New World Publishing, 2001.

MAGAZINES, JOURNALS, NEWSPAPERS, ETC.

Article from a magazine, journal, or newspaper with no author given:

"Uncovering Singapore's Past." <u>Montreal Globe and News</u> 16 Nov. 2004: B12.

"Singapore Grows Up." <u>Business Weekly</u> 7 Feb. 2003: 22–24.

Article from a magazine, journal, or newspaper with one or more authors:

Crawford, James. "The Fall of Singapore." <u>Straits News</u> [Singapore] 21 Jan. 2005: 5.

Yeo, Jeannette, and Lee Goh. "The Future of Singapore." <u>This Week in News</u> 9 Jan. 2003: 72.

Review of book, movie, film, or product:

Poh, Harry. Rev. of <u>Singapore: History and Geography</u>, CD-ROM, Harris Technology. <u>Computer Magazine</u> Aug. 1999: 19.

Nguyen, Katherine. "The Singapore Way." Rev. of <u>Singapore: The Movie</u>, dir. Marcus James. <u>National Review</u> [Singapore] 11 Nov. 2001: C6.

GOVERNMENT DOCUMENT

Singapore. Minister of Economic Affairs. <u>Singapore's Economic Outlook: May 2004</u>. Singapore: Minister of Economic Affairs, 2004.

United States. National Council on American-Asian Affairs. <u>Promoting United States-Singapore Relations</u>. Washington: GPO, 2001.

INTERVIEW

Long, Helstrom. Personal interview. 21 July 2006.

FILM, AUDIO, OR TV

Film or video recording:

<u>The Singapore Story</u>. Dir. Amy Shaw. Perf. Vince Tan. DVD. HBO, 2005.

<u>A Simple Life</u>. Dir. Nick Yan. Writ. Jim Son. Perf. Mort Smith and Ming Won. Videocassette. Universe, 1999.

Audio recording:

Yan, Alex. <u>Curry and Ginger</u>. Tokyo. Audioworks, 1996.

Television or radio:

<u>Lance Kwan Live</u>. SNews, Singapore. 27 May 2004.

<u>Lee Kuan Yew Speaks</u>. WSON, Houston. 6 Oct. 2002.

COMPUTER SOFTWARE

<u>Singapore: A Multimedia Tour</u>. CD-ROM. Los Angeles: PCTools, 1998.

INTERNET

"Singapore: A Brief History." <u>Historic Information Services</u>. May 2000. 9 Apr. 2006 <http://www.his.org /sing2000.html>.

THAT'S NOT ALL, FOLKS!

Remember that bibliographies are listed in alphabetical order by author (or title if no author is given). The list above is *not* in the correct order. If the sources listed above were your complete bibliography, it would be organized like this:

Brinker, Bob. The Story of Singapore. Toronto: Asian Press, 2002

Caan, Jacques, et al. The Politics of Southeast Asia. San Francisco: Heath Inc., 1998.

Chen, Andrea, and K.M. Granada, eds. The Merlion's Shadow. Hong Kong: Second Chance Publishing, 1996.

Crawford, James. "The Fall of Singapore." Straits News [Singapore] 21 Jan. 2005: 5.

Dart, Richard, and Michelle Nolan. Singapore. Singapore: Binding Press, 2004.

Greene, John, ed. Singapore Heat. Los Angeles: Smith Publishing, 1994.

Lance Kwan Live. SNews, Singapore. 27 May 2004.

Landis, Manny, et al., eds. The Birth of the Singapore Nation. New York: Melvin's Press, 1995.

Lee Kuan Yew Speaks. WSON, Houston. 6 Oct. 2002.

Long, Helstrom. Personal interview. 21 July 2006.

Nguyen, Katherine. "The Singapore Way." Rev. of Singapore: The Movie, dir. Marcus James. National Review [Singapore] 11 Nov. 2001: C6.

Poh, Harry. Rev. of Singapore: History and Geography, CD-ROM, Harris Technology. Computer Magazine Aug. 1999: 19.

Preston, Landry B. "Singapore: History." New World Encyclopedia. 2002 ed. New York: New World Publishing, 2001.

A Simple Life. Dir. Nick Yan. Writ. Jim Son. Perf. Mort Smith and Ming Won. Videocassette. Universe, 1999.

"Singapore: A Brief History." Historic Information Services. May 2000. 9 Apr. 2006 <http://www.his.org /sing2000.html>.

Singapore: A Multimedia Tour. CD-ROM. Los Angeles: PCTools, 1998.

"Singapore." Encyclopedia of Southeast Asia. 1998 ed. Boston: Freedom Press, 1997.

"Singapore Grows Up." Business Weekly 7 Feb. 2003: 22–24.

Singapore. Minister of Economic Affairs. Singapore's Economic Outlook: May 2004. Singapore: Minister of Economic Affairs, 2004.

The Singapore Story. Dir. Amy Shaw. Perf. Vince Tan. DVD. HBO, 2005.

The 2005 Guide to Singapore. New York: Charles Publishing Group, 2005.

"Uncovering Singapore's Past." Montreal Globe and News 16 Nov. 2004: B12.

United States. National Council on American-Asian Affairs. Promoting United States-Singapore Relations. Washington: GPO, 2001.

Yan, Alex. Curry and Ginger. Tokyo. Audioworks, 1996.

Yeo, Jeannette, and Lee Goh. "The Future of Singapore." This Week in News 9 Jan. 2003: 72.

Yew, Lee Kuan. The Autobiography of Lee Kuan Yew. Trans. M.E. Heller. Chicago: Bandera, 1999.

CHAPTER 10
USING A FRESH SET OF EYES

So many student writers get through writing their research paper and then think, "Whew! I'm glad that's over!" They turn in their papers and get them back, graded much lower than they thought they deserved. Then they look over the graded paper, finding sentences that don't sound right, spelling and grammar mistakes, and perhaps more. They think, "My paper wasn't this sloppy when I wrote it! How did this happen?" Does this sound familiar?

So many writers feel like the work is done with the first draft of the research paper. The hard truth is that usually the first draft is not a writer's best work. Writing requires review and revision. After all, why would we call it a first draft if there were no second draft?

When you finish your first draft, don't immediately start reviewing your paper. You have to transition from being in the writing zone. Your ideas are still in the front of your mind. Reviewing and revising right now will probably result in a lot of missed errors. Why?

Writers know what they *meant* to say. They know what the *intended* message was. So when they read their papers right after writing them, they might skim over the material instead of reading it thoroughly. At this point, writers don't see the actual words they wrote but rather what they *meant* to write.

In order to do a good review, you need to read your paper as if you have never seen it before. Read it slower. Try to be objective and see if your writing makes sense. Look for places that you could make the writing clearer. Then be prepared to do it all over again!

HOW MANY REVISIONS DOES IT TAKE?

It takes what it takes. In other words, you may need to revise a few times to get your paper in its best shape. You may want to read through the paper once for meaning, and then a second time to make sure your changes are better than your original writing. Then you can read your paper through for grammar, usage, and mechanics issues. Then you should read through one more time to make sure your paper fulfills the entire assignment given by your teacher. That doesn't count any reading you ask other people to do for you as well. Yes, that's a lot of rereading, but it makes all the difference in getting the grade you want.

In general, reviewing and revising is done in two phases. The first phase is to look at the thesis. In this phase, your concern should be how well you support your thesis. You should be sure your sentences are clear, your paragraphs are well written, and your paper is organized properly. The second phase is proofreading. In this phase, you should be looking for grammar, mechanics, and usage issues. You should also use the proofreading phase to make sure your citations (endnotes, footnotes, bibliography) are correctly written. Don't try to handle both phases at the same time. It's too much to look for together, and you are likely to miss mistakes that you would spot if you took the extra time to review in these two distinct phases.

READY, SET, WAIT!

So we've convinced you to take the time to revise your paper. Now we will ask you to wait. Take a day off. At the very least, sleep on it. The distance in time will help you clear your head of the ideas you have been writing and let you look at the paper with a fresh eye. This means you need to plan for the downtime in your schedule, but trust that it's worth the wait.

This may well be a good time to ask a peer or parent to read over your paper. You can ask for comments to be written in the margin of the paper, especially to note where the paper may not make sense or needs further clarification.

DON'T BITE THE HAND THAT FEED(BACK)S YOU!

Getting feedback from someone is a great way to improve your writing. Unfortunately, feedback inherently comes with criticism. You have to learn not to take it personally. Look at the comments as a chance to correct problems and clarify your ideas. Chances are, if the person you have review your paper doesn't understand what you are saying, neither will your teacher.

NOW GET STARTED!

After you take the break from your paper, get serious about revising. There is no one correct way to go about it. Go through the suggestions in this chapter and try them. See which ones work for you and follow through. There are four basic things you can do when you revise: add, remove, move, and change. Read on to find out more.

ADD

You may find places in the paper where you need to add information. If you find that your explanation isn't very clear, then you probably would benefit from adding some writing.

REMOVE

You may have written too much about a single point in some parts of the paper. If you find yourself thinking, "Enough already!" it may be time to cut some text from your paper.

MOVE

As you read your paper, there may be sentences and paragraphs that seem out of place. You can try moving the information around to see if it reads better or makes more sense.

CHANGE

If you find yourself reading the same dull words and phrases, then consider changing your words. A thesaurus can help you find better, more interesting ways to say what you are trying to convey.

Whether you are revising for meaning or proofreading, all of your changes will fall under one of these four categories. Now the trick is simply finding those mistakes!

GENERAL SUGGESTIONS

One excellent technique for finding problems in your paper is to read it aloud. It forces you to read slower, which writers sometimes have trouble with. Reading the paper aloud also lets you hear what any other reader would hear. If you have trouble reading the paper clearly, that's a clue that the sections that are awkward may need revising.

Use a sheet of paper or a ruler to focus your reading on one line at a time. It will keep your eye from wandering over words that are already very familiar to you.

When it is time to proofread, read the paper backward. Start at the end and read one sentence at a time. This removes a lot of the meaning from the paper so that you can focus on sentences, words, and punctuation.

If at all possible, write every draft of your paper on a computer in a word-processing program. It is easier to read, so poor or tired handwriting is not an issue. You are more likely to notice spelling and punctuation errors in typed text. You can also set the computer to print the paper double- or triple-spaced, with extra room on the sides. This will allow you plenty of room to mark up the paper as you make revisions.

SO CAN I JUST REVISE ON THE COMPUTER?

We don't recommend you revise your paper on the computer. There are many studies that have concluded that people revise poorly on a computer compared to on paper. This may be because you only see a small part of the paper at once. It could also be because writers depend too much on the computer to find errors for them.

That's not to say you should *not* use the computer's editing tools. Just use them in addition to your own revision and proofreading. Here is how to make the best use of the electronic proofing tools.

SPELL-CHECK

Spell-checkers are great tools, but you should understand how they work. Word processing software has a built-in dictionary. It compares each word in the document against the words in the dictionary. If it can't find a match, the software thinks the word is misspelled. So technical or specialized words may not be spelled wrong, but the computer thinks they are because they are unfamiliar. In addition, if you misspell a word in a way that happens to be another word, then the computer will not mark it as wrong. This is a strong reason to proofread for spelling on your own in addition to using the computer. Spell-checking should be a habit. For example, you should always run the spell-check before you print.

USING THE SEARCH AND REPLACE FEATURE

All word processing programs have a find and replace command that you can use to look for any word, phrase, or punctuation in a document. Use the find and replace command to find errors such as misused words or phrases. For example, maybe you often confuse the words *capitol* and *capital*. You can find the incorrect word and replace it with the correct one.

If you happen to make common mistypes on the computer, the find and replace command can help with this as well. For example, if you often type *loose* instead of *lose*, you can search for your common misspelling and correct it.

DETAILED REVISION SUGGESTIONS

The rest of this chapter will cover specific things to look for in your papers. You can refer to the appropriate chapters to refresh your memory about any particular topic. You may wish to read through your paper one time for each category to be sure you review your paper thoroughly.

CONTENT

Does your title give a good idea of what your paper is about? Remember, "Research Paper" is *not* a good title! (Chapter 7)
Is there an attention-getting introduction? (Chapter 7)
Is your thesis statement clearly stated in the introduction? (Chapters 2 and 7)
Does every paragraph have something to say about the thesis? (Chapter 7)
Have you used enough examples to make your ideas clear? (Chapter 7)
Have you avoided faulty reasoning in any argument? (Chapter 3)
Does the conclusion give the reader something to think about? (Chapter 7)

ORGANIZATION

Does the organization match the type of paper you wrote? (Chapter 3)
Can the reader clearly identify the introduction, body, and conclusion? (Chapter 7)
Is your sequence logical? (Chapter 3)
Do you use transition words to move from one idea to the next? (Chapter 3)
Does each paragraph in the body of your paper have a topic sentence? (Chapter 7)

Does each paragraph have information that is needed to explain or defend your thesis? (Chapter 7)
Do you avoid introducing new information in your conclusion? (Chapter 7)

RESEARCH AND SOURCES

Do you use quotations, paraphrases, and summaries correctly? (Chapters 5, 7, 8, and 9)
Are your footnotes/endnotes and bibliography in the style your teacher assigned? (Chapters 8 and 9)
Are your sources authoritative? (Chapters 3 and 5)
Is the research unbiased? (Chapter 5)
Have you written your own comments for each piece of research included? (Chapter 7)
Have you checked the direct quotations against the original source? (Chapter 3)
Do quotations flow in the paper seamlessly? (Chapter 7)
If material was paraphrased, are the sources included in the bibliography? (Chapter 9)

STYLE

Do you use different verbs throughout the paper? (Chapter 7)
Do you use too much passive voice? (Chapter 7)
Do you use a variety of sentence structures and lengths? (Chapter 7)
Is your choice of words clear and concise? (Chapter 7)

PROOFREADING

Proofread on paper, using proofreader's marks to save time. (Appendix)
Do all subjects and verbs agree? (Chapter 11)
Are the verb tenses consistent? (Chapter 11)
Are your sentences free of sentence fragments and run-ons? (Chapter 11)
Do your pronouns agree with the words they substitute? (Chapter 11)
Is all capitalization correct? (Chapter 11)
Is all spelling correct? (Chapter 11)
Is all punctuation correct? (Chapter 11)

TEACHER-SPECIFIC CHECKS

Is the assignment complete?
Do you use the margins, font, etc., that your teacher may have required?
Is the information appropriate for the assignment?

CHAPTER 11
WRITE IT RIGHT!

After all your hard work researching and writing, it would be a shame to get marked down because of sloppy Language Arts skills. So this chapter is devoted to things like grammar, punctuation, capitalization, spelling, and tricky words. Use this chapter as a reference for common problem areas. Read it through, and use it as a guide for your revisions that are covered in Chapter 10.

CAPITALIZATION

This table gives some basic rules for capitalization. If you have a question about whether a specific word should be capitalized that doesn't fit one of these rules, check a dictionary to see if the word is capitalized there.

Capitalize this. . .	But not this. . .
The first word of a sentence A roller coaster is made up of a series of connected cars that move on tracks.	No exceptions
The pronoun *I* The last time I rode a roller coaster was in 1997.	No exceptions
Proper nouns The last roller coaster I rode was the Greased Lightning at Astroworld.	No exceptions
Titles that come before names The engineer who designed the roller coaster was Professor Anne James.	**Titles that come after names** She is the sister of Paul James, professor of English.
Words used as proper nouns I rode in the front car with Uncle Tom.	**Words *not* used as proper nouns** None of my other uncles would ride with us.

Capitalize this. . .	But not this. . .
Specific religious words I sat in front of a man that looked like Buddha.	Nonspecific use of the word *god* The ride was named after a mythological god.
Direction words that are part of names This is the largest roller coaster on the West Coast.	Direction words that are not part of names It travels from east to west.
Days of the week, months of the year, holidays The ride opened on Halloween, which is the last day in October.	No exceptions
Seasons as part of a name They called the opening celebration the Fall Festival.	Seasons in general They close the ride down for winter.
Names of cultures and languages The cars were painted in traditional American colors.	No exceptions
The first letter of quotations that are complete sentences My uncle said, "This is a very intense ride!"	The first letter of quotations that are not complete sentences I asked him what he meant by "intense."
The first word in a title A Call to Arms	No exceptions
The rest of the words in a title The Thin Man	Small articles and prepositions in the rest of the title The Wizard of Oz
Periods of time and historic events People at the festival were dressed as if it were the Great Depression.	Century numbers Everything looked like it did in the early twentieth century.

PUNCTUATION

This section explains the basics of using the most common punctuation marks.

APOSTROPHES

Apostrophes are used to show ownership. For singular nouns, and plural nouns that don't end in *s*, add an *'s*. For plural nouns that end in *s*, just add an apostrophe.

> The roller coaster's inertia holds it to the track. The passengers' screams were deafening. The women's screams were the loudest.

Apostrophes make plurals of letters, numbers, and words that are used as words.

> The conductor had people count off by 1's and 2's. When he asked who was ready, all we heard were yes's.

Apostrophes are used to take the place of missing letter in contractions.

> We couldn't wait any longer for the ride to start.

COLONS

Use a colon to introduce a quotation of two sentences or more.

> The engineer asked: "Does the inertia of a body depend upon its energy content? Let's find out."

Use a colon to introduce a list of items *not* following a verb or preposition.

> We will discuss the design of three well-known American roller coasters: the Riddler's Revenge, the Boomerang, and the Canyon Blaster.

Use a colon to separate hour from minute in the time.

> The ride ended at 3:17 P.M.

COMMAS

Use a comma to separate items in a list or series.

> You must understand inertia, gravity, potential energy, and kinetic energy to know how coasters run.

Use a comma to separate two adjectives before a noun if the adjectives express different ideas.

> Wooden roller coasters provide a bumpy, noisy ride. Newer steel coasters have smoother rides.

Use a comma after introductory phrases in a sentence.

> Once the coaster starts moving downhill, the potential energy changes to kinetic energy.

Use a comma to set off interrupters.

> Some tubular steel rides, however, have cars suspended from the tracks.

Use a comma to separate the month and day from a year.

The park opened its newest ride on April 7, 2004.

Use a comma to separate city and state.

The ride was built at Six Flags in Dallas, Texas.

DASHES

Use a dash to show the reader that a thought is changing midsentence.

The ride grew bumpy—the brakes were slipping.

Use a dash to show a surprising element at the end of a sentence.

They discovered the best seat on the ride—the front seat.

ELLIPSES

Use an ellipsis to show that words or sentences have been deleted.

The review described the roller coaster as "an amazing accomplishment. . . that seems to defy the rules of physics."

HYPHENS

Use a hyphen to join two words together to show one adjective.

It turned out to be an ill-conceived design.

Use a hyphen to show that a word is continued on the next line. Place the hyphen between syllables.

The chain pulled the twenty cars up the incline until it reached the crest of the track.

PARENTHESES

Use parentheses to show figure and table citations.

The curve resembles a parabola (Figure 4).

Use parentheses to introduce abbreviations and acronyms.

The speed of the cars is measured in miles per hour (mph).

SEMICOLONS

Use semicolons to separate items in a list if the items contain commas.

The engineers created rides with long, smooth inclines; sharp turns; and loops that turned passengers upside down.

Use a semicolon to join two related, independent clauses in one sentence.

The ride was a success; the company would build three more just like it.

IT'S CLEAR AS MUD: USING PRONOUNS CLEARLY

Pronouns are words that take the place of nouns. (Think of words like *I, we, he, she, it, you,* and *they.*) There are a few rules to keep in mind so that the pronouns you use are clear to the reader.

Pronouns should agree in number. Singular nouns are matched with singular pronouns. Plural nouns are matched with plural pronouns:

The ride was great.   The rides were great.
It was great.   They were great.

Pronouns should agree in person. For example, if you are writing in the first person (*I* or *we*), don't switch and start using the second person (*you*) or third person (*he, she, they, it*).

Pronouns should clearly refer to the noun they are replacing. A rule of thumb is that the pronoun replaces the noun that comes closest before it.

Pronouns are either subjective or objective. Use subjective pronouns in the place of subjects, and use objective nouns in the place of objects.

RELAX! VERB TENSES AREN'T TOO BAD!

Good writers keep the same tense in their writing throughout their papers. This isn't too difficult to do, except you have to know all of the oddball verbs that you might want to use. First, let's review the different tenses, and then give a list of those difficult verbs so that you'll be able to use them correctly.

There are three basic tenses: past, present, and future. The past tense tells about something that already happened. Present tense tells about something that is happening now. Future tense tells of something that will happen. So for a simple verb, the three tenses look like this:

Verb	Past Tense	Present Tense	Future Tense
to save	I saved He saved	I save He saves	I will save He shall save

For these regular verbs, you can almost always decide which to use by thinking about the time (past, present, or future) and saying the verb in a sentence. You can tell when the verb sounds correct or not by saying it out loud as part of a sentence.

You can also add a helping verb (have, has, or had) to a verb to make *perfect* tenses. In these cases, the main verb is always past tense, but the helping verb changes among past, present, and future tense. So the same verb, in perfect tenses, would look like this:

Verb	Past Perfect Tense	Present Perfect Tense	Future Perfect Tense
to save	I had saved She had saved	I have saved She has saved	I will have saved She shall have saved

Finally, you can write verbs in past and present participles. The present participle form of the verb has an *-ing* ending. It usually is written with words like *are, is, be,* etc. The past participle looks like past tense but might be written with words like *has.* So here are the participles:

Verb	Past Participle Tense	Present Participle Tense
to save	It has been saved	They are saving

So for simple verbs, if you know the past, present, and future tenses of verbs, you can then write all eight ways that might come up (past, present, future, past perfect, present perfect, future perfect, past participle, and present participle). Whew!

So to stay consistent in writing your paper, make sure you use the same tense. Generally speaking, you should be using past, past perfect, and past participle tense together, and present, present perfect, and present participle tense together.

WHY NOT THE FUTURE?

You won't see a research paper written in future, future perfect, or future participle tense. Why? Research is inherently based on what has already happened. You can't study and report on something that has not yet happened. So you can imagine it would be difficult to create an entire paper around a thesis that hasn't yet occurred!

NOW FOR THE WEIRD ONES

The weird verbs, called *irregular verbs*, have unusual past and past participle forms. Regular past-tense verbs end in *-ed*. So do their past participles. Irregular verbs don't follow the same rule. So here is a nice, long chart of many irregular verbs and their weird ways. Keep an eye out for them in your writing to make sure you have written them correctly.

Verb	Present	Past	Past Participle
to arise	arise(s)	arose	arisen
to awake	awake(s)	awoke *or* awaked	awaked *or* awoken
to be	am, is, are	was, were	been
to bear	bear(s)	bore	borne *or* born
to beat	beat(s)	beat	beaten
to become	become(s)	became	become
to begin	begin(s)	began	begun
to bend	bend(s)	bent	bent
to beset	beset(s)	beset	beset
to bet	bet(s)	bet	bet
to bid (*to command*)	bid(s)	bade	bidden
to bid (*to offer*)	bid(s)	bid	bid
to bind	bind(s)	bound	bound
to bite	bite(s)	bit	bitten *or* bit
to bleed	bleed(s)	bled	bled
to blow	blow(s)	blew	blown
to break	break(s)	broke	broken
to breed	breed(s)	bred	bred
to bring	bring(s)	brought	brought
to broadcast	broadcast(s)	broadcast	broadcast
to build	build(s)	built	built
to burn	burn(s)	burned *or* burnt	burned *or* burnt
to burst	burst(s)	burst	burst
to buy	buy(s)	bought	bought
to cast	cast(s)	cast	cast
to catch	catch(es)	caught	caught
to choose	choose(s)	chose	chosen
to cling	cling(s)	clung	clung
to come	come(s)	came	come
to cost	cost(s)	cost	cost
to creep	creep(s)	crept	crept
to cut	cut(s)	cut	cut
to deal	deal(s)	dealt	dealt
to dig	dig(s)	dug	dug
to dive	dive(s)	dived *or* dove	dived
to do	do(es)	did	done
to draw	draw(s)	drew	drawn
to dream	dream(s)	dreamed *or* dreamt	dreamed *or* dreamt
to drink	drink(s)	drank	drunk
to drive	drive(s)	drove	driven
to eat	eat(s)	ate	eaten

Verb	Present	Past	Past Participle
to fall	fall(s)	fell	fallen
to feed	feed(s)	fed	fed
to feel	feel(s)	felt	felt
to fight	fight(s)	fought	fought
to find	find(s)	found	found
to fit	fit(s)	fit	fit
to flee	flee(s)	fled	fled
to fling	fling(s)	flung	flung
to fly	flies, fly	flew	flown
to forbid	forbid(s)	forbade *or* forbad	forbidden
to forget	forget(s)	forgot	forgotten *or* forgot
to forgive	forgive(s)	forgave	forgiven
to forego	forego(es)	forewent	foregone
to forsake	forsake(s)	forsook	forsaken
to freeze	freeze(s)	froze	frozen
to get	get(s)	got	got or gotten
to give	give(s)	gave	given
to go	go(es)	went	gone
to grind	grind(s)	ground	ground
to grow	grow(s)	grew	grown
to hang (*to suspend*)	hang(s)	hung	hung
to have	has, have	had	had
to hear	hear(s)	heard	heard
to hide	hide(s)	hid	hidden
to hit	hit(s)	hit	hit
to hold	hold(s)	held	held
to hurt	hurt(s)	hurt	hurt
to keep	keep(s)	kept	kept
to kneel	kneel(s)	knelt	knelt
to knit	knit(s)	knit *or* knitted	knit *or* knitted
to know	know(s)	knew	known
to lay	lay(s)	laid	laid
to lead	lead(s)	led	led
to leap	leap(s)	leaped *or* leapt	leaped *or* leapt
to learn	learn(s)	learned *or* learnt	learned *or* learnt
to leave	leave(s)	left	left
to lend	lend(s)	lent	lent
to let	let(s)	let	let
to lie (*to rest or recline*)	lie(s)	lay	lain
to light	light(s)	lighted *or* lit	lighted or lit
to lose	lose(s)	lost	lost

Verb	Present	Past	Past Participle
to make	make(s)	made	made
to mean	mean(s)	meant	meant
to meet	meet(s)	met	met
to misspell	misspell(s)	misspelled *or* misspelt	misspelled *or* misspelt
to mistake	mistake(s)	mistook	mistaken
to mow	mow(s)	mowed	mowed *or* mown
to overcome	overcome(s)	overcame	overcome
to overdo	overdo(es)	overdid	overdone
to overtake	overtake(s)	overtook	overtaken
to overthrow	overthrow(s)	overthrew	overthrown
to pay	pay(s)	paid	paid
to plead	plead(s)	pled	pled
to prove	prove(s)	proved	proved *or* proven
to put	put(s)	put	put
to quit	quit(s)	quit	quit
to read	read(s)	read	read
to rid	rid(s)	rid	rid
to ride	ride(s)	rode	ridden
to ring	ring(s)	rang	rung
to rise	rise(s)	rose	risen
to run	run(s)	ran	run
to saw	saw(s)	sawed	sawed *or* sawn
to say	say(s)	said	said
to see	see(s)	saw	seen
to seek	seek(s)	sought	sought
to sell	sell(s)	sold	sold
to send	send(s)	sent	sent
to set	set(s)	set	set
to sew	sew(s)	sewed	sewed *or* sewn
to shake	shake(s)	shook	shaken
to shave	shave(s)	shaved	shaved *or* shaven
to shear	shear(s)	shore	shorn
to shed	shed(s)	shed	shed
to shine (*to glow*)	shine(s)	shone	shone
to shoe	shoe(s)	shoed	shoed *or* shod
to shoot	shoot(s)	shot	shot
to show	show(s)	showed	shown *or* showed
to shrink	shrink(s)	shrank	shrunk
to shut	shut(s)	shut	shut

Verb	Present	Past	Past Participle
to sing	sing(s)	sang	sung
to sink	sink(s)	sank *or* sunk	sunk
to sit	sit(s)	sat	sat
to slay	slay(s)	slew	slain
to sleep	sleep(s)	slept	slept
to slide	slide(s)	slid	slid
to sling	sling(s)	slung	slung
to slit	slit(s)	slit	slit
to smite	smite(s)	smote	smitten
to sneak	sneak(s)	sneaked *or* snuck	sneaked *or* snuck
to sow	sow(s)	sowed	sowed *or* sown
to speak	speak(s)	spoke	spoken
to speed	speed(s)	sped	sped
to spend	spend(s)	spent	spent
to spill	spill(s)	spilled *or* spilt	spilled *or* spilt
to spin	spin(s)	spun	spun
to spit	spit(s)	spit *or* spat	spit
to split	split(s)	split	split
to spread	spread(s)	spread	spread
to spring	spring(s)	sprang *or* sprung	sprung
to stand	stand(s)	stood	stood
to steal	steal(s)	stole	stolen
to stick	stick(s)	stuck	stuck
to sting	sting(s)	stung	stung
to stink	stink(s)	stank *or* stunk	stunk
to stride	stride(s)	strode	stridden
to strike	strike(s)	struck	struck
to string	string(s)	strung	strung
to strive	strive(s)	strove	striven
to swear	swear(s)	swore	sworn
to sweep	sweep(s)	swept	swept
to swell	swell(s)	swelled	swelled *or* swollen
to swim	swim(s)	swam	swum
to swing	swing(s)	swung	swung
to take	take(s)	took	taken
to teach	teach(es)	taught	taught
to tear	tear(s)	tore	torn
to tell	tell(s)	told	told
to think	think(s)	thought	thought
to thrive	thrive(s)	thrived *or* throve	thrived
to throw	throw(s)	threw	thrown

Verb	Present	Past	Past Participle
to thrust	thrust(s)	thrust	thrust
to tread	tread(s)	trod	trodden
to understand	understand(s)	understood	understood
to uphold	uphold(s)	upheld	upheld
to upset	upset(s)	upset	upset
to wake	wake(s)	woke or waked	waked or woken
to wear	wear(s)	wore	worn
to weave	weave(s)	weaved or wove	weaved or woven
to wed	wed(s)	wed	wed
to weep	weep(s)	wept	wept
to win	win(s)	won	won
to wind	wind(s)	wound	wound
to withhold	withhold(s)	withheld	withheld
to withstand	withstand(s)	withstood	withstood
to wring	wring(s)	wrung	wrung
to write	write(s)	wrote	written

COMING TO AGREEMENT: SUBJECTS AND VERBS

Another common problem writers run into is subject-verb agreement. For simple sentences, making the subject and verb agree usually is pretty simple. The trouble comes with compound subjects or verbs. Also, some words look singular when they are plural, or the other way around. So let's start simple and work our way through the more complicated combinations of subjects and verbs.

Singular subjects get singular verbs. Most singular verbs end in -s or -es.

The girl climbs.

Plural subjects get plural verbs. Remove the -s or -es and your verb is generally plural.

The girls climb.

THE EXCEPTION TO THE RULE

As with other parts of the English language, there are exceptions about how to make singular and plural verbs. When in doubt, check the dictionary, as it usually shows how the verb is used.

When the subject is two or more nouns or pronouns connected by *and*, use a plural verb.

The girls and boys climb.

When the subject is two or more singular nouns or pronouns connected by *or* or *nor*, use a singular verb.

> The girl or boy climbs.

When a subject has both a singular and a plural noun or pronoun connected by *or* or *nor*, the verb agrees with the part of the subject that is closest to the verb.

> The girls or boy climbs.
> The girl or boys climb.

Don't pay attention to phrases that come between the subject and verb when deciding if the verb is singular or plural.

> One of the girls climbs.

In sentences that start with *there is* or *there are*, the subject comes after the verb. Make sure the verb agrees with the subject that comes after it.

> There are many girls climbing.
> There is a boy climbing.

There are also a few subjects where you may have trouble deciding if they are singular or plural. This table should help:

Singular Subjects		Plural Subjects
each	someone	scissors
each one	no one	tweezers
either	civics	trousers
neither	mathematics	shears
everyone	measles	pants
everybody	news	
anybody	team	
anyone	committee	
nobody	group	
somebody	family	

Finally, don't get tricked by phrases with words like *including, as well as,* and *in addition to*. Look only at the subject. If it is singular, the verb is, too. If the subject is plural, so is the verb.

BITS AND PIECES: SENTENCE FRAGMENTS

Writers sometimes write so fast they don't realize that their sentences are incomplete. These incomplete sentences are called *sentence fragments*.

Sentence fragments either have a subject or a predicate, but not both. Remember that the subject tells who or what the sentence is about. The predicate tells what happens with the subject. Look at this sentence:

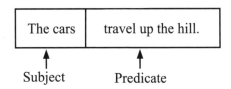

The cars is the subject because it tells who the sentence is about. *Travel up the hill* tells what happens to the cars, so that is the predicate. Subjects have a noun or a pronoun (*cars*). Predicates have a verb (*travel*). There may be other words and phrases, but there must at least be the noun and the verb.

So a sentence fragment is missing the subject, the predicate, or even both. Sentence fragments might look something like this:

> Then turns the corner.
> At the bottom of the ride.

The simple correction is to rewrite the sentence to include the subject and the predicate.

> Then the car turns the corner.
> The kinetic energy drops at the bottom of the ride.

TOO MUCH INFORMATION: RUN-ON SENTENCES

Writers sometimes put too much information in a sentence by including more than one complete idea. This usually happens when the writer uses the wrong punctuation or no punctuation at all. When two or more sentences are written as one sentence, this is called a *run-on*.

Here are some examples:

> Safety engineers ride the coaster, they are looking for problem areas.

The new idea starts here. The comma should be a period.

> What you see while riding the coaster makes you feel like you are going faster designers make sure you see the loops and turns coming.

A new idea starts here. This should be two sentences, not one.

To correct a run-on sentence, simply break the sentence into two properly written sentences, with punctuation and capitalization. The run-on sentences above would look like this when they are corrected:

Safety engineers ride the coaster. They are looking for problem areas.

What you see while riding the coaster makes you feel like you are going faster. Designers make sure you see the loops and turns coming.

DON'T ABUSE YOUR LANGUAGE!

There are more than a few words and phrases in the English language that trip up writers. Some sound alike; others are used in similar circumstances. Many writers choose the wrong words or phrases, making them sound less intelligent. English teachers seem to be always on the lookout for errors like these.

So below is a list of some of the most-often confused words and phrases along with examples of how they should be used. The list is not complete, as every writer has different words that he or she finds confusing. If you have a concern about a word you are using, check the dictionary.

ACCEPT OR EXCEPT?

accept: to receive. *The designers accepted an award for the roller coaster design.*
except: to exclude. *Everyone rode it except my mother.*

ADVICE OR ADVISE?

advice: a recommendation. *The doctor gave me good advice.*
advise: to offer a suggestion. *I would advise you to take another road.*

AFFECT OR EFFECT?

affect: to influence. *The rain will affect the safety of the ride.*
effect: result. *The effect of the rain was devastating.*

AID OR AIDE?

aid: to help. *The nurse was able to aid the paramedics.*
aide: an assistant or helper. *The nurse's aide works part-time.*

ALLUDE OR ELUDE?

allude: to make an indirect reference to something. *The engineer alluded to a problem with the brakes.*
elude: to escape or avoid detection. *The problem with the brakes eluded the repairman.*

AMONG OR BETWEEN?

among: used with three or more persons or things. *I could not decide among the four rides which to go on first.*
between: used with two persons or things. *I could not decide between the wooden and steel roller coasters, so I rode both!*

BAD OR BADLY?

bad: an adjective that means not good or correct in any way. *The reviews of the new park were bad.*
badly: an adverb used to describe how poorly or unsatisfactorily something is done. *The rails were badly welded together.*

BECAUSE OR SINCE?

because: a reason or cause for something. *The ride closed because of poor weather.*
since: a period of time. *The ride has been closed since the rain started.*

BESIDE OR BESIDES?

beside: next to. *The book is beside the television.*
besides: in addition to. *Besides, I want to go away to college.*

CAN OR MAY?

can: to be physically or mentally able to do something. *I can reach the bar now that I am taller.*

may: to have permission to do something. *You may ride that roller coaster one more time.*

CAPITAL OR CAPITOL?

capital: wealth; the city that is the seat of the government; an uppercase letter. *The ride required a lot of capital. The capital of Illinois is Springfield. All titles start with a capital letter.*

capitol: a building housing the seat of the government. *The state health-care meeting was held in the capitol.*

COMPLEMENT OR COMPLIMENT?

complement: the completeness or the process of supplementing something. *The fast music complemented the ride.*
compliment: praise. *The park owner received compliments for the renovations.*

DUAL OR DUEL?

dual: double. *The car has a dual-exhaust engine.*
duel: to fight. *The knight challenged the prince to a duel.*

IT'S OR ITS?

it's: a contraction of *it is* or *it has*. *It's the longest ride in North America.*
its: the possessive of the pronoun *it*. *The coaster reached its maximum speed.*

LAY OR LIE?

lay: to put something or someone down. *I lay my jacket on the seat.*
lie: to rest or recline. *I went to lie down after the ride.*

LOOSE OR LOSE?

loose: not contained or tight. *Her hair came loose from the clip.*
lose: to fail to win; to fail to keep possession of. *I don't want to lose that gold coin.*

PRINCIPAL OR PRINCIPLE?

principal: the head of a school; important. *The principal moved some books out of her office.*
principle: a truth or law. *The lawyer talked about the principles of the case.*

THAN OR THEN?

than: used for comparison. *I am older than your brother.*
then: at that time. *I would like to talk to you then.*

THEIR, THERE, OR THEY'RE?

their: possessive form of the word *they*. *Their ride travels over seven hills.*
there: at or in that place. *The new ride is over there.*
they're: contraction of the words *they* and *are*. *They're building another ride.*

TO, TOO, OR TWO?

to: toward. *We can walk to the zoo.*
too: also. *Your friends can come along too.*
two: the number after one. *I have two extra tickets.*

WEATHER OR WHETHER

weather: atmospheric conditions. *Have you heard what the weather will be like tomorrow?*
whether: if. *I need to know whether it will be hot enough to swim.*

WHO'S OR WHOSE?

who's: the contraction of *who* and *is*. *Who's cooking dinner tonight?*
whose: the possessive of *who*. *Whose sock is this?*

YOU'RE OR YOUR?

you're: contraction of the words *you* and *are*. *You're afraid to go on the ride.*
your: a possessive form of *you*. *This is your favorite ride.*

COMMONLY MISSPELLED WORDS

Just as many writers confuse the same words and phrases, writers often misspell the same words. So the last section of this chapter is a list of some very commonly misspelled words. Again, if you aren't sure of the spelling of a word and it is not in this list, check a dictionary.

a lot	accommodate	advertise
abscess	acquaintance	again
absence	acquire	agreeable
abundance	acquit	all right
accelerate	adamant	allege
acceptable	admirable	always
accidental	adolescent	amateur

analyze	caught	deterrence	friend
ancient	cemetery	different	gauge
annulled	changeable	dilemma	governor
anoint	clothes	disagree	grateful
anonymous	collaborate	disappear	grievous
antecedent	collectible	discernible	guarantee
anxious	colonel	discipline	guess
anyone	colossal	disheveled	gullible
appalling	column	dissimilar	happily
apparent	commitment	dumbfound	harass
appearance	committed	ecstasy	height
arguable	committee	eighth	heresy
argument	compelled	eligible	hierarchy
arrival	complement	embarrass	humorous
assess	concede	energy	hypocrisy
bachelor	conceited	enforceable	ignorance
battalion	concurred	enough	immediate
beautiful	conscience	equipment	independent
believe	conscientious	exceed	indispensable
besiege	consensus	excise	inflexible
biscuit	contemptible	exercise	innocuous
bookkeeper	coolly	exhilarate	innuendo
brief	copyright	existence	insistence
broccoli	corroborate	experience	intelligent
brought	counterfeit	facetious	irascible
bureau	cousin	favorite	irresistible
caffeine	criticize	feign	jewelry
calendar	decisively	fierce	judgment
campaign	deficient	financier	kernel
cannot	definite	foreign	khaki
captain	demagogue	forfeit	leisure
category	desirable	forty	liaison

library	omitted	reign	supersede
license	oppressive	relevance	suppress
lightning	orator	relief	surprise
livable	parallel	repetition	susceptible
loneliness	passable	repressible	sustenance
maintenance	pastime	restaurant	synagogue
manageable	people	resuscitate	tariff
maneuver	perceive	retained	thoroughly
medieval	perseverance	revise	threshold
memento	personnel	rhyme	tobacco
merchandise	plausible	rhythm	tongue
millennium	playwright	satellite	traceable
miniature	possession	schedule	trespass
minimize	precede	secession	twelfth
miniscule	preference	seizure	tyranny
miscellaneous	preferred	sensitive	unskillful
mischief	presumptuous	separate	until
mischievous	privilege	sergeant	usable
misspell	proceed	sheriff	usually
misstate	profited	shield	vacancy
movable	prohibited	shriek	vacillate
necessary	pronunciation	sieve	vacuum
negligible	publicly	sincerely	valuable
neighbor	questionnaire	skepticism	villain
newsstand	quizzed	sovereign	weird
noticeable	quotient	specify	wholly
obscene	rarefy	stationery	wield
obsession	receive	succumb	withhold
occasional	receipt	suddenness	worshipper
occurred	recommend	sufficient	yield
occurrence	referred	superintendent	

PROOFREADING SYMBOLS

This chart, taken from Merriam-Webster's, provides all the proofreading symbols you'll need to proofread your research papers.

Symbol	Meaning	Example
ℰ or ✄ or ✐	delete	The brown sad dog sleeps. ✄
⌣	close up	Don't with hold information. ⌣
℘	delete and close up	close up ℘
∧ or ⟩ or ∧	insert	insert∧ here *word*
#	insert a space	put one∧here #
eg #	space evenly	space∧evenly∧where∧ indicated *eg #*
stet	let stand	let marked ~~text~~ stand as set *stet*
tr	transpose	change ͜order the͜ *tr*
/	used to separate two or more marks and often as a concluding stroke at the end of an insertion	The brown sad dogs sleeps∧ ✄/⊙
⌐	set farther to the left	⌐ too far to the right
⌐	set farther to the right	too far to the left ⌐
⌒	set as ligature (such as æ)	encyclopa͡edia
≈	align horizontally	ali͡gnment
//	align vertically	// align with surrounding text
×	broken character	imperf͜ect ×
⊓	indent or insert em quad space	∧list ⊓ *em*
¶	begin a new paragraph	¶ The brown dog sleeps.
ⓢⓟ	spell out	set ⟨5 lbs.⟩ as five pounds ⓢⓟ
cap	set in CAPITALS	set <u>nato</u> as NATO *cap*
sm cap or s.c.	set in SMALL CAPITALS	set <u>signal</u> as SIGNAL *s.c.*

Symbol	Meaning	Example
lc	set in lowercase	set $\cancel{S}$outh as south *lc*
ital	set in *italic*	set <u>oeuvre</u> as *oeuvre* *ital*
rom	set in roman	Set as Times New Roman *Regular* *rom*
bf	set in **boldface**	Set as Times New Roman <u>Bold</u> *bf*
= or -/ or $\overset{\frown}{\smile}$	hyphen	multi$_\wedge$colored =
$\frac{1}{N}$ or <u>en</u> or /N/	en dash	1965$_\wedge$72 $\frac{1}{N}$
$\frac{1}{M}$ or <u>em</u> or /M/	em (or long) dash	Now—at last!$_\wedge$we know. $\frac{1}{M}$
V	superscript or superior	$\overset{V}{}$ as in $\pi r2 =$ as in πr^2 $\overset{V}{}$
∧	subscript or inferior	$\overset{\wedge}{}$ as in H20 = as in H$_2$0 $\overset{\wedge}{}$
$\hat{V}$ or $\overset{V}{\wedge}$	centered	for centered dot in $p_\wedge q$ $\langle\rangle$
$\wedge$	comma	Trenton$_\wedge$NJ $\wedge$
$\overset{V}{}$	apostrophe	St. Johns$_\wedge$is a hospital. $\overset{V}{}$
⊙	period	St. John's is a hospital$_\wedge$ ⊙
; or ;/	semicolon	Juan wants to visit his uncle$_\wedge$;/ however, he has made no plans.
: or ⊙	colon	The following$_\wedge$ ⊙
$\overset{V}{}\overset{V}{}$ or $\overset{V}{}\overset{V}{}$	quotation marks	^{V}This guy...^{V}Lucas said. $\overset{V}{}\overset{V}{}$
(/)	parentheses	—*Publishers Weekly*^{V}starred review^V (/)
⊏/⊐	brackets	The AWF$_\wedge$African Wildlife Foundation$_\wedge$works to protect the ⊏/⊐ wildlife in Africa.
ok/?	query to author: has this been set as intended?	The waves were high that day. *ok/?*
℗	turn over an inverted letter	inve$_\wedge$rted ℗
wf	wrong font	wrong si$_\wedge$Ze or st$_\wedge$yle *wf*

CHAPTER 12
GET THE GRADE

Teachers have a variety of methods to use in order to grade a research paper. We will give the most common examples here. If you understand what typical teachers look for, then you can be sure to gear your paper toward the grade you want to earn.

NUMBER GRADES

One way teachers can grade a research paper is with a number grade from 0 to 100. In order to come up with a number grade, teachers usually assign points to different aspects of the paper.

Prewriting [10 points]

Writer shows evidence that he/she has considered ideas and their support.

Writer submits an outline and at least **one rough draft** in addition to the final, clean copy.

Organization and Development [50 Points]

Writer creates a well-developed introduction that moves from general to specific information.

Writer states the essay's thesis as the last sentence of the introduction.

Writer composes a topic sentence for a body paragraph when introducing a new subtopic from the thesis statement.

Writer **fully** develops each body paragraph by using facts, details, examples, and specific textual references taken from a close reading of the assigned literary selection.

Writer uses transitions within and between paragraphs to organize logically the essay's information and to achieve coherence throughout the essay.

Writer begins the conclusion with a reminder of the thesis statement.

Writer composes the paper's last sentences to bring closure to the essay's central idea.

Writer follows MLA format for the composition's final copy, which includes parenthetical documentation of outside resources when used and a "Works Cited" page listing those outside resources.

Since this section is worth the most points to this teacher, you should focus your revisions here first.

Style [20 points]

☐ Central Idea

Writer presents a significant and interesting central idea, clearly defined and supported with substantial, concrete, and consistently relevant details.

☐ Sentence Structure

Writer skillfully constructs sentences that display fluency, economy, and effective variety.

☐ Diction

Writer uses diction that is appropriate to the essay's subject, purpose, audience, and occasion; it is distinctive in precision, economy, and the idiomatic use of English.

There aren't 20 separate things in this section to earn 20 points. The teacher decides how much each checkbox is worth.

Mechanics and Usage [20 points]

Capitalization	Punctuation	Spelling
Pronoun usage	Pronoun/antecedent agreement	Verb tense
Subject/verb agreement	Adjective/adverb usage	Word meaning
Omission of words	Misplaced/dangling modifiers	Other

Teachers who assign number grades may have systems of checklists that vary from this one a bit, but you get the idea. It can be very helpful to know the grading system as you write. If at all possible, get a copy of the grading checklist *before* you turn in your final paper. It can give you another view to use in writing your final draft.

LETTER GRADES

Some teachers do not want to spend the time pouring over every little detail of a class's batch of papers. To simplify grading, the teacher may choose to simply assign a letter grade: A, B, C, D, or F. The teacher still needs to use a scale of some sort in order to assign grades. The scale may look like this:

A—EXCELLENT

An *A* essay includes all the characteristics of *B* and *C* work as well as the following:

_____ The writer offers an insightful thesis.

_____ The writer consistently offers clear and detailed explanations in support of the thesis.

_____ The reader has no doubt how the writer arrived at the conclusions offered.

_____ The sources are an integral part of the essay, incorporated smoothly into the flow of the writing.

_____ The essay is easy to read because it flows smoothly from idea to idea.

_____ There are few or no errors in grammar, mechanics, etc.

_____ The writer has made good use of language.

B—GOOD

A *B* essay includes all the characteristics of *C* work as well as the following:

_____ The writer has a more specific, focused thesis.

_____ The sources aren't just there but help to advance the argument.

_____ The writer consistently offers better explanation and support for the how and why of the definition.

_____ The paper is better organized, making good use of transitions and other signals to the reader about the direction of the essay.

C—ADEQUATE OR COMPETENT

A *C* essay demonstrates the writer's ability to communicate ideas and has these characteristics:

_____ The writer has a clear thesis.

_____ The essay offers some explanation of how the writer arrived at the thesis.

_____ The essay offers some explanation of why the ideas are important to the writer.

_____ The essay is controlled by the thesis; while the essay diverts from topic occasionally.

_____ The writer makes use of two to four sources.

_____ The sources are correctly documented and integrated into the wording of the essay with signal phrases.

_____ The paper has a clear organization that doesn't leave the reader wondering where the essay is headed.

_____ The paper has no consistent problems with grammar, mechanics, spelling, punctuation, or sentence structure.

D—INADEQUATE OR INCOMPETENT

D work falls short of three or more of the requirements for *C* work, and/or it may reflect the following:

_____ The writer failed to meet the requirements of the assignment.

_____ The paper contains consistent problems with grammar, mechanics, spelling, punctuation, or sentence structure that hinder the reader's progress through the essay.

_____ The organization of individual paragraphs is problematic.

_____ The organization of the overall essay is problematic.

F—COMPLETELY UNACCEPTABLE OR FAILING

An *F* paper shows problems with content, structure, and mechanics. This writing is characterized by any of the following: unclear purpose; incoherent organization; inadequate, irrelevant, or illogical development; little originality of thought; reliance on clichés; inappropriate word choice; ineffective or incorrect sentence structure; numerous or significant problems with mechanics and grammar. Plagiarism is also grounds for failure.

You can see that the letter grade system requires less intense scrutiny by the teacher but still scores the writing on those concepts that are most critical to good paper-writing. Some teachers may extend the letter grades by assigning +'s and −'s to the letters. A writer could earn an A+, A, A−, and so on.

RUBRICS

A popular way to score student writing is using a rubric. A rubric is simply a way to categorize papers. Truthfully, the letter grade system above is a type of rubric, because the papers are categorized by letter. The newer rubrics that you might see are based on a number score that is usually *not* 100. Every teacher's rubric can look completely different from the next. Here is one example:

	4 Excellent	3 Very Good	2 Good	1 Fair	0 Poor	Total
Quality of Content (Double points for this section)	A thorough paper; the assigned topic area was included, ample research both pro and con was included, all information presented was factually correct, and analysis and conclusions were justified.	A good paper; the assigned topic area was included, some research both pro and con was included, few if any factual errors were made, and analysis and conclusions were justified.	An adequate paper; the assigned topic area was included, some research both pro and con was included, a few minor factual errors were made, and analysis and conclusions were appropriate.	A fair paper; the assigned topic area was included, scant research was presented, some factual errors were made, and analysis and conclusions were flawed.	Little was written, scant or no attention was paid to research, factual errors were made, and analysis and conclusions were either missing or not justified.	0–8
Organization	The paper had an obvious beginning and ending; was very well organized and easy to follow.	The paper began and ended satisfactorily; the paper was mostly well organized and easy to follow.	The beginning or ending of the paper were fair; overall the paper's organizational structure was passable.	The beginning and ending were weak; organizational structure was lacking.	The beginning and ending were confusing; information was very disorganized.	0–4
Mechanics and Style	MLA format was correctly followed; no grammatical or spelling errors; overall, the paper was very well written.	MLA format was almost always correctly used; no or few grammatical errors were made; overall, the paper was well written.	MLA guidelines were inconsistently followed; a few grammatical and/or spelling errors were made; overall, the paper was acceptably written.	MLA guidelines were inconsistently used; several grammatical and/or spelling errors were made; overall, the paper was not well written.	The MLA guidelines were not used; grammatical and/or spelling errors were frequently made; overall, the paper was poorly written.	0–4
Organizational Component	A well-developed outline and rough draft were submitted.	An outline and rough draft were submitted.	An incomplete outline and/or rough draft were submitted.	Either the outline or rough draft were missing.	No outline or rough draft were submitted.	0-4
Grand Total						0–20

You can see that a rubric is a faster grading system, much like the letter grade system. The benefit of the rubric is that it is presented in a very organized way, so it's a very fast way to assess a paper. As a student, the rubric can help you as you write, as you can see where to focus your attention. In this case, you would want to be sure to get the outline and rough draft turned in, as those are an easy 4 points. Then your focus would be on writing a quality paper, ensuring that you follow MLA style, and proofreading your paper thoroughly.

YOUR FINAL PAPER

At this point, you should be done with your research paper! Your paper should have a good flow of words and ideas. Your organization should make sense and suit the type of paper you have written. You can find transitions between ideas and paragraphs. The paper also credits the sources you used for your research in the form of footnotes or endnotes as well as a bibliography. Pat yourself on the back—you did it!